$34.95

The Daily Art of Management

THE DAILY ART OF MANAGEMENT

A Hands-On Guide to Effective Leadership and Communication

PEG THOMS

JAMES F. FAIRBANK

PRAEGER

Westport, Connecticut
London

Library of Congress Cataloging-in-Publication Data

Thoms, Peg, 1948—
    The daily art of management : a hands-on guide to effective leadership and
    communication / Peg Thoms and James F. Fairbank.
        p. cm.
    Includes bibliographical references and index.
    ISBN 978–0–275–98961–3 (alk. paper)
1. Management. 2. Leadership. 3. Communication. I. Fairbank, James F. II. Title.
HD31.T496   2008
658—dc22   2008000215

British Library Cataloguing in Publication Data is available.

Library of Congress Catalog Card Number: 2008000215
ISBN: 978–0–275–98961–3

First published in 2008

Praeger Publishers, 88 Post Road West, Westport, CT 06881
An imprint of Greenwood Publishing Group, Inc.
www.praeger.com

Printed in the United States of America

The paper used in this book complies with the
Permanent Paper Standard issued by the National
Information Standards Organization (Z39.48–1984).

10 9 8 7 6 5 4 3 2 1

I would like to dedicate this book to all of the terrific managers with whom I have worked over the years including, but not limited to, Jerry Converse, Dan Miller, Garth Garlock, Lisa Turner, Donna Kraus, and John McFarland. These are some of the folks who have set high standards and provided good examples of management during my working career.

—Peg Thoms

I dedicate this book to the best manager I have ever known: my wonderful wife, Jacki. In addition to managing our family and our home, she has accomplished the delicate and nearly impossible task of managing me.

—Jim Fairbank

Contents

ONE

Moving Statues

It is easier to get people to move a statue than to move a stone. If you understand this concept and can apply it, you do not need this book. If you do not understand it, we have written this book to help you better manage other people in organizational and group settings.

Most managers have studied leadership and management in some form—perhaps a college course as an undergraduate student or a corporate training program held either in-house or at an off-site seminar that cost your organization thousands of dollars. Despite the time and money spent on this type of training and education, we continue to hear horror story after horror story about ineffective or inappropriate day-to-day management behavior. We have been waiting years for things to change, but they have not.

We wrote this book as a guide to teach managers how to behave in specific day-to-day situations. It will describe common functions performed by managers at various levels and explain how each type of situation should be handled. If managing others is not a natural instinct for you, this book can help. If you did not learn good communication styles growing up, this book can help. If you have not had the opportunity to observe effective managers in your work life, this book can help. If you were an excellent worker, but find yourself to be a mediocre or poor leader, this book can help.

If you thought management would be easy, but it isn't, this book can help you.

In a recent interview,[1] Dr. Jo Anne Van Tilburg was asked why the natives of Easter Island carved the giant stone statues **before** moving them several miles to the locations they would be displayed (for hundreds of years). This was an important question because the statues often broke along the way and new stones had to be carved and moved again.

To the practically minded manager, this doesn't make any sense. Her response was simple, yet prolific. These fifteenth century tribal leaders realized that it was easier to get people to move statues than stones due to the cultural and societal significance of a statue. A stone, on the other hand, is simply a stone. Technically, could the leaders have forced followers to move a stone? Perhaps! By means of threatening, killing, torturing, promising redemption, or ostracizing those who refuse, leaders can force followers to do anything—up to a point. But the best way to motivate, accomplish difficult tasks, and maintain power is to engage followers in meaningful activities. Therein lies the problem. How does a leader get followers engaged in tedious day-to-day tasks? How does one convince others that moving a statue (especially one that glorifies the leader) weighing thousands of pounds is in their best interests?

Like all trendy ideas made up by management gurus, the term "meaningful activity" sounds simple, but it is not easy to implement in practice. Many Americans have boring tasks to perform that will never be meaningful. Nonetheless, things like emptying trash, typing memos, and copying and packaging software must be done. Even higher-level tasks like long-range planning become tedious over the years.

If you are desperate to become a better manager or organizational leader, you may have read the latest books. Here are some recent admonitions by management and leadership experts:

1. You have been told that you ought to get a vision, but you don't even know what that is let alone how to "get" one.
2. You have heard that it is valuable to eliminate boundaries in your organization (called "boundarylessness"), but boundaries

are strictly maintained by the very people telling you to rid your unit of them.

3. You have been encouraged to become "intrapreneurial"—entrepreneurial in a corporate setting—in your organization and told that creativity is important, but the last time you tried something different, you were embarrassed and reprimanded by a member of senior management.

4. You have been advised to rank order all of your subordinates and fire the bottom 10 percent. However, you like the bottom 10 percent because they do their jobs well, even though they are not quite as good as the top 10 percent. Besides that, you find it increasingly difficult to hire good replacements.

5. You have been told that self-leadership is the key, but you are clueless as to what that means even after reading numerous books on this subject.

6. You know from reading the experts that charisma is important, but you don't have it—so why even bother?

7. You have been told that younger workers are different—maybe lazy or maybe smarter—but you find that they are just like all other workers except that they aren't afraid of computers.

8. You have been taught to "benchmark," to quantify everything that you do, essentially "Six Sigma" your way to corporate success, which should be measured by a "Scorecard." However, you know that it only takes one stray employee to derail all of your work and that of your entire organization. You realize that you are helpless to prevent that type of behavior, and that knowledge has made you paranoid.

9. You know that you should be empowering subordinates, but you wonder how that differs from delegating and self-managed teams—concepts which were advocated twenty years ago and have since all but disappeared from the business lexicon.

Advice today is coming from college football coaches, religious leaders, former CEOs (some of whom were fired for performance reasons), Genghis Khan (supposedly), *The Art of War*, one minute managers, leadership "pipeline" experts, and, of course, your dad who does not understand why you attend all of your children's soccer games instead of working through them (and dinner most nights) as he did. Instead of helping managers with day-to-day leadership, this advice is nonspecific and general, providing little practical information which can be put into action.

Many managers have also studied theories of management, leadership, and organizational behavior. You may once have been able to explain them or pass a test on them, but today you most likely could not put the instrumentality piece of Expectancy Theory[2] into practice if your life depended on it. For what it is worth, we have had well-published academics tell us that they couldn't put their own research findings into practice. In other words, you may still understand a theory you once learned, but have no idea how to apply it in a work setting. One of our favorite stories is of the respected business school dean who was acknowledged as a leading expert on leadership and management who found himself outside his own office, with a sobbing secretary inside, after a performance review. He had no idea how to get back into his office.

Before you let your mind wander off on a tangent about "ivy covered walls" and "ivory towers," let us share another story. When conducting management training twenty years ago in a financial services company, a vice president of investments was given an article by a leading management expert. Before even reading the article, the VP commented, "Articles on management by college professors remind me of men who write books on sex, but have never been with women." Although the comment was certainly funny and illustrates stereotypes about college professors, the VP had to be reminded that there is something far worse—men who have made love to fifty women but have yet to please one. Managers, who have "done it" for twenty years, may or may not know any more than the professor who never "did it." Like it or not, academic types have a few things to teach managers and managers have a few things to teach professors. We are asking you to set aside your biases about university professors, worthless management training you have attended in the past, poor managers you have known, young people, old people, and other different people who report to you. In the end, it turns out that people, despite the distinctly different times and environments in which they are raised, are very similar in terms of what motivates them to be productive.

This book was specifically designed to help you manage more effectively on a day-to-day basis. Here is our plan for the book:

Chapter 1 has introduced the purpose of the book and what you can expect to learn.

Chapter 2 will provide you with a concrete method of developing and communicating a vision for a small work department or an entire organization, a social club or a children's sports league, or a church or a regional professional association.

Chapter 3 will teach you how to develop and write organizational, departmental, and individual goals. An emphasis will be placed on development of challenging goals and measurement approaches. It will also explain how you can ensure achievement of the goals.

Chapter 4 will help you create an ethical work environment. This chapter will focus on the ethical treatment of employees as well as customers. Aside from the corporate ethics handbook, managers set the tone for socially responsible behavior and learning to model the desired behavior is critical.

Chapter 5 will provide a step-by-step plan for recruiting and hiring the right people. This is the most important task that managers complete. Too often, managers try to motivate workers after they are hired instead of hiring people motivated to do the work on the front end.

Chapter 6 will show you how to communicate effectively in various types of situations. At least half of the challenge of communicating effectively is understanding who to tell what. Managers have a tendency to either say too little or to say too much to followers who have no need to know. We will provide guidance on how to decide what to tell, whom to tell, and how to tell.

Chapter 7 will help you understand motivation of subordinates. This will include a number of specific strategies from work design to sharing food. We will suggest a range of techniques which can be easily and quickly implemented in most work settings. In addition, this chapter will focus on conducting the performance appraisal. This is another difficult management task. Providing ongoing feedback on performance is one of the most critical skills for a manager. We will help you identify the appropriate feedback and how to conduct a useful performance evaluation.

Chapter 8 will provide an overview of organizational change. All leaders know how difficult it can be to make changes between people and systems that resist change as much as possible. The development of change plans depends on the scope and the nature of the desired change. We will help you diagnose the type of change you want to implement, and the best approach to that change.

Chapter 9 will provide a thorough summary of how to understand and deal with competition. Strong successful managers enjoy their competition—they learn from them and become better in order to continue to produce the best services and products. We will show you what your competitors can do for you, how to monitor their strategies, and how to continue to improve and stay in the game.

Chapter 10 focuses on the development of positive public relations—how managers can affect the perceptions of others in their market regarding their personnel and products. We will talk about handling emergencies, becoming the best place to work, maintaining good buzz about your organization, and meeting problem situations head on.

Chapter 11 will demonstrate the value of being a solid citizen on both the personal and professional level. Community leadership is part of the job of an effective manager. It is a way to improve the business environment, meet the people essential to your organization, and discover community needs which might be met through community service or through your organization's products.

Chapter 12 will encourage you to begin to utilize the strategies described in earlier chapters while creating more effective teams in your department or organization. We do not advocate teams as a substitute for managers, but rather as one of the many effective tools available to you. You can learn to move statues in order to increase earnings and create memorable experiences for members of your organization.

If you are hoping that this book will provide you with one slogan, gimmick, or shortcut to management, put it down. There is no such thing as managing in one minute. There are more than seven habits that you must develop and they are not always common sense. Management is only a war if you make it one. The skills that make one a coach of great athletes will not help you become a better manager. The stories are not cute, action filled, or suspenseful. Managing effectively is hard work requiring the mastery of a variety of specific business skills and the use of well-developed management techniques. Management work is often repetitive, tedious, and frustrating. In the end, however, you will achieve more in less time with greater efficiency. You will make more money, feel more successful, and have followers who respect you.

NOTES

1. J.A. Van Tilburg, Interview on The Today Show, November 7, 2005.

2. V.H. Vroom, *Work and Motivation* (New York: John Wiley & Sons, 1964).

TWO

Creating an Organizational Vision

Vision is not a new topic. The concept, if not the exact term, has been used since prehistoric man (at least since the modern human brain evolved) and is known in most cultures. (For a better understanding of the role of vision throughout history and across cultures, see David Maybury-Lewis'[1] *Millennium: Tribal Wisdom and the Modern World*.) Vision recently emerged in the leadership literature as an essential element of transformational and charismatic leadership.

For many years, leadership researchers had been looking for the "secret" to leadership by using traditional scientific methods. Finally, a new approach to research on leadership emerged—qualitative or descriptive research. With this approach, behaviors have been identified that are consistently characteristic of effective leaders. The one behavior that is found over and over again in these studies is creating and communicating organizational vision. It would be fair to say that creating a positive organization vision is one of the most important behaviors of effective leaders of organizations which must change.

Research indicates that some people are more future oriented, more positive, and more optimistic than others. These are all traits with environmental, situational, and genetic roots. What we know for sure is that some of us create positive images of our organizations and ourselves in the future. These images drive our behavior. This is part of our nature. We do it without thinking. Unfortunately, many humans are incapable of imaging a future for their organizations that is brighter than today's reality without some assistance.

There is help for those people, however, because research also suggests that visioning can be learned and practiced. It may never be as easy for some as it is for others, so many managers will have to remind themselves to do it. You probably know if you do this automatically or if you will need to force yourself to focus on this type of behavior.

An organizational vision is a cognitive image of the future. It must be positive enough to followers to motivate them and elaborate enough that it provides direction for future planning and goal setting. A vision is not a prediction of the future—accurate predictions are based on the past. A vision is what we intend to create. Note that we define vision as a cognitive image which suggests that it can never be shared in whole with followers. It exists in the mind of the leader and in the minds of the followers in the forms that make it acceptable or unacceptable to each. Effective leaders will change unacceptable visions or leave their organizations to create or lead an organization which has the potential to achieve a more consistent (with the leader's values, beliefs, and personal goals) vision. Followers will be drawn to leaders and organizations which have visions in which they believe, or they will leave to find better fits for themselves when it is possible.

There are numerous examples of transformational leaders and their visions. For example, consider the following leaders and their visions of the future:

- Nelson Mandela—to end apartheid in South Africa.
- Anita Roddick (founder of The Body Shop retail chain)—to create a profitable and socially responsible company.
- Bill Gates—a computer in every home.
- Tecumseh—unite Native American tribes against European settlers.
- Martin Luther King Jr.—"I Have a Dream."

It is important to understand that dreams don't always come true in the form in which they were created. The point is that humans get further when the vision is of an ideal situation. There are a number of explanations for how and why organizational visions work.

1. A vision sits at the top of an individual's or an organization's hierarchy of goals answering the question, "Why am I (or why are we) doing this?" Vision drives an individual's behavior. If that individual happens to be a leader of an organization, he/she must communicate all or part of his/her vision to others and hold them accountable for achieving their piece of the vision.

2. A vision tends to motivate followers because it makes them think about a positive future. If the followers are not future oriented, it makes the future seem closer which makes them more likely to act. If followers are not positive about the organization, themselves, or life in general, a positive vision can make them feel better.

3. A vision is a self-fulfilling prophecy. If people believe that something is true or is likely to happen, they will behave in ways that confirm that belief.

4. A vision develops commitment. We understand where the organization is going and get to decide if we want to go along. When we stay (or are hired knowing what the vision is), we are more committed.

5. A vision directs planning and behavior—it provides direction.

6. A vision is a deal struck between a leader and the constituents of the organization. These constituents may be customers, employees, stockholders, the community, etc. All parties are committed to keep their end of the deal.

7. A vision is a type of "strategic thinking." Mintzberg[2] suggested that strategic thinking begins with the possibilities, the ideal, and what we can become in the future as opposed to the limitations of the organization and trends in the industry.

There is a difference between a vision, a mission, a philosophy, and a vision statement.

The mission is the reason that we exist or our primary purpose. For example, the mission of a church is to provide spiritual guidance and support to its members. The mission of a school is to educate children in a community.

The philosophy is the set of beliefs that guide both the mission and the daily business of the organization. For example, a Unitarian church may be an appropriate resource for individuals who do not share the beliefs of more traditional types of religion but are seeking the community support system that a church typically provides. A private school may have teachers and administrators who believe that each child's learning must be individualized instead of being organized around traditional grade levels.

A vision statement is a brief summary of what an organization hopes to achieve in the future. Usually, this summarizes the mission and philosophy. Generally, these vision statements are posted in a hallway or highlighted in an annual report. They tend to look very much like every other organization's "vision" and are usually a waste of time. These statements have been the butt of many Dilbert[3] jokes.

True visions are different from vision statements in that they are colorful, elaborate, and exist in the minds of the leaders. The vision has to be complex and detailed in order to provide direction. It has to be open to change, but not compromise. There is a difference.

A number of approaches have been used to create an organizational vision over the years including fasting, drugs, torture, self-mutilation, isolation from others, and, worst of all, strategic planning retreats where executives escape as quickly as possible to the golf courses. The problem with these approaches is that some are illegal and/or not healthy and the last one doesn't work.

Many experts insist that we need to develop a "realistic" vision—something highly valued in traditional management. Strategic planning approaches to visioning incorporate the same lists of limitations and trends that strategic planners employ. This approach ties us to the past and present. It does not open doors to the future. Visions must be idealistic to work.

Here is an approach that incorporates strategies used to increase creativity. It leads to a positive, idealistic, and complex vision. Essentially, it involves three steps. Let's look at each separately.

STEP 1: CREATING A CLUSTER TO REFLECT THE COMPLEXITY

A vision must include every aspect of the organization to be comprehensive enough to direct behavior. In order to achieve that, we place the name or type of organization in the center of a large sheet of paper. For example, assume that it is fifty years ago and you are Walt Disney. You want to create an amusement park. You don't want it to be like the typical parks found at Coney Island or Cedar Point. You want it to be unique, highly entertaining, profitable, and relate to your business.

Put the words "Amusement Park" in the center of a large piece of paper.

Begin to identify each aspect of an amusement park that you can think of on the board.

As you begin to identify related elements, draw lines to show their connections. How the various elements are connected is less important than getting them all down on paper. You want to make sure that you have everything covered. Each person involved in the process (if the leader does it alone it will only include his/her ideas) will make different connections. Figure 2.1 shows how this will begin to look. Note that each connection may have dozens of connections that are subsets of it. This becomes a large complex network or "web" of key elements which should find their way into the vision.

Now, practice this step on your own. Think of an organization of which you are a part. Don't use your work group or organization to start. You can use your church, your daughter's soccer league, your golf club, your civic group, or any organization in which you are involved. Create a cluster for that group. Put the name of it in the middle of a sheet of paper and begin Step 1. Remember that at this stage, you are simply trying to identify each element that is part of or must be considered in an organization.

STEP 2: CREATING THE IDEAL

Once you have created the cluster, the next step is to list *"Wouldn't it be great if..."* statements for every element of the cluster

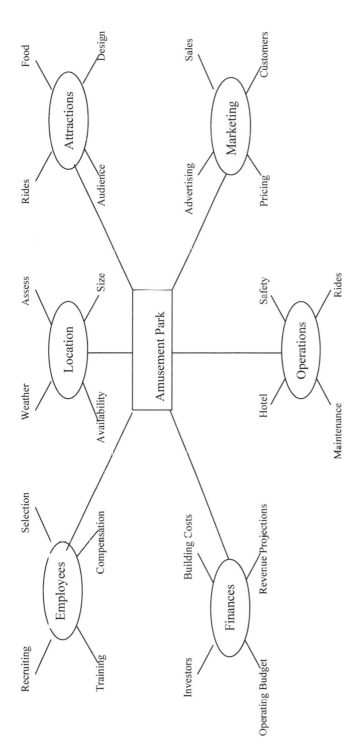

Figure 2.1 Step 1—clustering.

you have created. In order to help you understand this process better, go back to the amusement park. Here are some examples which Walt Disney might have used in creating his vision:

- *Wouldn't it be great if* our park would be appealing to people of all ages?
- *Wouldn't it be great if* the weather were good year round at our park?
- *Wouldn't it be great if* our cartoon characters worked at the park?
- *Wouldn't it be great if* we could charge immense sums of money for admissions and people would pay it?
- *Wouldn't it be great if* there was never an accident in our park?
- *Wouldn't it be great if* visitors could tour the world while in our park?

Notice that these statements are idealistic. That is the point! Go for the ideal even when if it sounds silly or self-serving. Because we are familiar with Disneyland and Disney World, this exercise is a bit easier than creating our own visions. When you create your own, focusing on the ideal scenarios will be more difficult. The ideal is scary to most of us either because we feel powerless, fear failure, or hear the inner voice saying, "Be realistic."

See if you can list ten more statements for the amusement park. To get ideas, look at the elements in the cluster in Figure 2.1.

Go back to the organization that you clustered before. List as many "Wouldn't it be great if..." statements as you can. Use your cluster to get ideas. We once knew an executive who used his golf club for his organization and he came up with, "Wouldn't it be great if I could skip the most difficult holes on the course?" Another used his son's soccer league and came up with one of the most seemingly silly ones of all time, "Wouldn't it be great if every child had fun?"

STEP 3: CREATING THE MOVIE IN YOUR MIND

Remember that a vision is nothing more than a cognitive image. You can think of it as a movie that you will play over and over in your mind. There are lots of movies in your mind now.

You use them for escape, for pleasure, to plan future activities, to rehearse your performance, and to review past events. This time, you are creating a movie of your ideal organization in your mind.

If you have been to Disneyland or Disney World, you have that movie in your mind and can play it now. What does it look, sound, smell, and feel like when you are there? Walk through the park. What do you see? What do you hear? What do you smell? What is good about it? Do you feel good?

Go back again to the organization you used for the personal exercise. Close your eyes. Imagine your organization two years from now if all of your "Wouldn't it be great if..." statements had come true. What would it be like? Imagine every detail. Allow time for this movie to play out and develop. If you see something which is not a good fit with the vision, change it. Picture the people involved. How do they look? Can you tell how they feel?

You may want to make notes as you watch your movie or create the script for the film. These notes can help you explain the vision to others, but remember that no one can have the exact cognitive image that you do.

STEP 4: USING THE VISION TO DRIVE STRATEGIC PLANNING

As we said earlier, the vision drives planning. Even items which appear to be very idealistic should become the goal and all constituents must begin to behave in ways to make the dream come true. Here are a few examples:

1. Suppose that Disney really did this activity and really asked, "Wouldn't it be great if cartoon characters worked at the park?" At Disney World, the cast members who play the cartoon characters are trained in the mannerisms and behaviors of the characters. The costumes are detailed and always in perfect condition. The park has built-in tunnels and hidden doors so that no cast member is ever out of costume in the public view. All of these things help the park come as close as possible to achieving this idealistic goal. Do real cartoon characters work

at the park? No. However, the park is far better off by starting with an idealistic goal than it would be if planning had begun by asking, "What kind of costumes should we have?" Do you see the difference it makes?

2. Imagine that you chose your child's soccer league as your organization. And suppose that one of your statements was, "Wouldn't it be great if every child had fun at every game?" That is a bit unrealistic, isn't it? Well suppose that we were going to develop the strategic plan and we used this idealistic goal to drive our planning. What could we do to make sure that every child had fun at every game? Our strategic plan may include things like:

   a. Offer alternative activities for children who don't like soccer,
   b. Don't keep score—for real,
   c. Don't allow parents to attend the games, or
   d. Arrange the team assignments and schedules based on the physical and mental development of the children instead of their ages and skill levels in the sport.

What we want to do is change the old rules and make new ones that will help us achieve our vision. So, if you think it would be great if you didn't have to play all the holes at your golf club, don't. You don't have too. Breaking out of conventional thinking in order to make the idealistic become reality is what vision is about. Obviously, we cannot break the law, but even laws can be changed. Our visions may even take us there. The bottom line is that an idealistic, positive vision takes us farther and to a different place than a realistic plan based on limitations and trends. Of course compromises will be required, but do not do this easily. Try as hard as you can to find real cartoon characters before you hire humans.

STEP 5: COMMUNICATING THE VISION TO OTHERS

Decide what parts of the vision should be communicated and to which people. Not everyone needs to understand the entire vision. Again, a cognitive image cannot be communicated in its entirety to others anyway. Financial institutions that will loan you the money to finance the vision need a certain type of information. Your advertising agency needs another. Your mother needs a different type. You will need a communication strategy for each constituent. Some constituents will need written information, others will require inspirational speeches that describe parts of the vision, and still others, will learn of your vision by watching your behavior. Here are a number of strategies to enhance the communication of your vision.

1. Incorporate the important parts of the vision into your daily communications and your major presentations regularly. Use the vision as the central theme every time you talk to others. Share the "dream," your "goal," what you "see in the future," or your "vision."
2. Model behavior consistent with your vision. If you want every employee to be customer friendly, others in the organization must see you serving customers. Live it. If you want subordinates to be diligent about quality, reread every memo containing your name and ensure that there are no errors.
3. Provide continuous feedback to others regarding their behavior and its consistency with your vision. Tell them if they are doing things that will help the organization achieve the vision. Tell them if they are not. Talk very specifically about the behavior and how it relates to the vision.
4. Use the vision to guide planning and goal setting. Every goal should lead to the vision (the mega-goal). Goal setting will be specifically described in Chapter 3.
5. Tie the vision to the values and goals of others. Show how achievement of the vision will help individuals achieve their personal goals.
6. Recruit and select employees whose values, beliefs, and personal goals are consistent with the vision.
7. Provide details on your vision when necessary—elaborate. Maybe someone is not performing or planning in a manner consistent with your vision. You may need to provide more elaborate information.

8. Use errors (gaps between the vision and performance) to teach. The more errors that are made, the more we learn when we get feedback.

9. Present the vision as a challenge. Tell people that you know that they are capable. "I know that you can do it." Understand that a very ideal part of the vision may be literally impossible, but get as close as you can and don't give up easily.

10. Use the vision to make the future seem closer.

11. Continuously monitor progress toward the vision. Involve others in the process.

12. When others ask why something is being done, point to the vision. If the vision doesn't answer the question, the task may be inappropriate.

13. The strategic plan should answer the question, "How will the vision be achieved?" Make sure that it does.

TEAMS VS. LEADERS IN THE DEVELOPMENT OF AN ORGANIZATIONAL VISION

Teams or groups can develop a vision using the same approach. However, it is impossible for every member of the team to share the same cognitive image. This needs to be understood and discussed among the group. If you want to use a group to develop a vision, do Step 1 together. Then do Step 2 as individuals. Come together later and create a laundry list of statements without any judging. This can even be done anonymously. Come back together and review the "Wouldn't it be great if..." statements that you are all willing to add. Write the script for the movie together along with a communication strategy.

THE IMPORTANCE OF LEADERSHIP

Many organizations are using participative styles of management. We tend to use groups to create visions, missions, philosophies, and goals. This approach to management is valuable in many situations. However, we believe in leadership. One person who incorporates a vision into his/her worldview can change an organization, or a community, or the world. A vision does not have to be approved by a committee. It exists independently in the mind of a leader. The leader must breathe life into the vision and select the right people to execute it.

FINAL EXERCISE

Using the steps that you have learned, create a vision for your work organization or department. However large your scope on the job is how large your vision should be. Take your time and develop an elaborate cluster, a comprehensive list of "Wouldn't it be great if...?" statements, and a detailed movie script. Then, develop the implementation and communication strategies.

NOTES

1. D. Maybury-Lewis, *Millennium: Tribal Wisdom and the Modern World* (New York: Viking, 1992).

2. H. Mintzberg, *The Rise and Fall of Strategic Planning* (New York: Free Press, 1994).

3. S. Adams, *The Dilbert Principle* (New York: Harper Collins, 1996).

THREE

Setting Organizational, Departmental, and Individual Goals

Goal-setting theory is not really a theory. It is a law of management—one which did not need to be legislated. If you are not currently setting personal goals and using performance goals to manage, you have missed the boat. Goal setting works.

What does it mean to say that goal setting works? It means that people do better work, do more work, persist longer at their work, and achieve more at work when they have specific challenging goals. Overall, research suggests that corporate performance (using bottom-line measures) is also substantially higher (as much as 40 percent) when goal setting is used. Summaries of the extensive goal-setting research can be found by entering the names of the leading experts in this field into a business or management search engine—Edwin A. Locke and Gary P. Latham. They have documented every study done on goal setting.

GOALS MAKE VISION A REALITY

Effective managers and leaders use goals to make their visions a reality. In other words, goals should answer the question, "How can we achieve our vision?" Performance goals, sales goals, and human resource goals tell the production, sales, and employment departments how they contribute to achievement of, for example, the CEO's vision of becoming the top quality R&D organization in their field. When goals of reducing production waste by 5 percent, increasing sales by 10 percent, and hiring ten of the top 100 chemical engineering Ph.D. graduates in a given year are met, the vision is more likely to become reality. Every person in the organization has a role in meeting the vision and their goals tell them what specific tasks must be achieved. Like the vision, goals should be challenging if they are to lead to the best performance.

There is a bit of confusion over the notion of goals because the term is often used interchangeably with the word "objectives." Essentially, they are the same for purposes of this book. MBO (Management by objectives) is an old strategy that encourages managers to link individual goals to organizational goals. This has rarely been done despite the extensive supportive research and the longevity of the concepts. Executives are very good at writing goals for subordinates, but not so good at creating a vision and articulating organizational goals to support it. What has usually resulted from MBO practices are lots of "loose" goals related to specific tasks performed on specific jobs which essentially create or duplicate job task performance standards. Although important, performance standards are not goals in the truest sense of the word. In cases where performance standards can be specified, they should be, and employees should be encouraged to achieve and exceed them, especially when quality can be enhanced. In addition to performance standards (or performance goals), specific goals should be set for other aspects of work and personal development.

Goals that do not answer the question, "How will the vision be achieved," may seem superfluous but they may be necessary to ensure day-to-day performance. Here is an example: In a large hospital, the Director of Medical Records set very high goals for timeliness and accuracy of information entered by transcriptionists into the medical records. However, she did not mention customer service. At that time, the medical transcriptionists had to leave their desks to locate and provide records to the health care professionals who used them. Meeting the quality and quantity goals for their jobs was more difficult when the transcriptionists had to interrupt their work to wait on a doctor who needed a medical record. Hence, the service provided at the medical records counter was slow and rude. The director had to add customer service performance goals. (Another solution would have been to add a clerk who did not transcribe medical records, but just pulled, delivered, tracked, and retrieved the records as needed.)

GOAL SETTING: BASIC PRINCIPLES

Writing goals is a difficult thing to do even though they appear to be simple on the surface. Also, there are a number of problems that can occur during the process. Following is a set of instructions and examples of goals. At the end of the chapter, we will discuss some of the problems that goals can create and how to solve those.

First, goals should be challenging; sometimes these are called stretch goals. The process by which goals work means that they develop commitment. The commitment to the goals is part of the reason that people work harder to meet their goals. In addition, people work harder when the goals are difficult. This is true whether the goal requires mental or physical effort, or both. People also tend to work longer and more persistently on challenging goals than they do on easy goals. If you are unsure about this, try this simple experiment. Ask five colleagues to list as many different uses of a coat hanger as they can. Tell them to do their best on this task. Ask a different group of five colleagues to list twenty different uses of a coat hanger. Calculate the average for each of the two groups. Nine times out of ten, the group given the specific and difficult goal of twenty uses will average two to four more, even though they may not meet the goal of twenty. This raises an important truism about challenging goals—they raise the level of performance even when they are not fully achieved. This seemingly paradoxical issue is one of the major causes of problems for managers, which is why we will return to it later in the chapter.

It is important that individuals believe that challenging goals are attainable. This causes many managers confusion because they do not know how to tell the difference between an easy goal and a challenging one. The best way to tell is by looking at the skill level and past performance of an individual. Each time one completes a task, the goal can be made more challenging the next time it is set. If it is too low the first time, the manager will see that it was fully achieved, ahead of time, with little effort. The next time, the deadline can be shortened. If a task is not completed on time or the quality is not sufficient, the deadline can be lengthened the next time and training on the task can be provided before the next project is begun.

Second, the coat hanger experiment demonstrates another rule about effective goal setting—goals should be specific. Research has found that the best goals are those that specify all of the criteria necessary to meet the goals. Notice how specific the following goals are:

- Twenty uses of a coat hanger,
- Ninety-five percent accuracy on the report data,
- June 1 deadline,
- Zero customer complaints during the first quarter,
- Zero rejected parts during the second half of the year,
- Ninety percent acceptance rate by reviewers.

Specificity is critical because it provides the means by which the individual and the manager know whether the goal was achieved. Most performance can be put into measurable terms. Think about how the work is typically evaluated. Maybe there are quantity and quality measures, sales goals, customer satisfaction surveys, rejection rates, and so on.

On occasion, there is work which is more difficult to specify. For example, how can you measure the performance of the advertising manager? If sales go down, does it mean the advertising was not effective? Not necessarily. However, the advertising can be evaluated in terms of its consistency with the marketing strategy, whether or not it met the budget, and reactions to the ads by experts in the field. Gathering feedback on performance from both internal and external audiences is something we need to seek. It can be critical to evaluating and improving performance.

Difficult and specific goals also indicate a manager's confidence in a subordinate. This confidence, when made public, provides an incentive to achieve the goals. This sends a message that the manager has faith in the ability of the employee. Asking for a lot is a compliment even though it is not always viewed as such. It is up to the manager to make sure the worker knows that challenging goals are a reflection of the worker's ability and the quality of previous work.

When bosses set easy goals, nonetheless, it is often done to lower their own work goals. In other words, if our subordinates have easy goals, our goals are more likely to be met, thereby increasing our chances for a raise. It is up to the boss' boss to make sure that the goals are challenging. Goal setting should start at the top, with the vision (which it rarely does in practice).

Ongoing feedback is also critical to goal completion. Feedback provides essential guidance and encouragement to the individual and shows the value that the manager places on the vision, the goal, and the individual's success. In combination, feedback, the manager's confidence in the individual, and the value placed on the goal can build the individual's commitment to the goal. Individual commitment to goals can also be developed when the individual understands the importance of the goals. In other words, whenever possible, workers should be assigned important tasks. If daily tasks are menial and simple, the worker must understand the role that she is playing in the overall performance of the organization.

There are exceptions to the rules regarding challenging and specific goals. In situations where an individual is lacking the knowledge to complete a task, a learning goal would be more effective than a specific performance goal. When one lacks the knowledge and skill to complete a task, he might be tempted to skip essential steps. The initial goal should be to learn the process. This can be followed by subgoals (smaller goals set for completion of the pieces or parts or stages of a larger task) and, eventually, by challenging goals once the task is learned and practiced.

EFFECTIVE GOAL SETTING

Let us look at an example of effective goal setting. Assume that Joe is a new salesperson of a specific type of equipment used in manufacturing. He is taking over the territory of a retired sales-person in June of 2008.

Goals for 1–3 Months of Employment

Goal 1: Joe will be able to pass a written test on the product and its use in manufacturing with a score of at least 90 percent by September 30, 2008. He will have retaken the test and earned a score of 98 percent by October 31, 2008.

Goal 2: Joe will have visited every current customer, including observation of their use of the product and lunch with each purchasing agent and/or manufacturing executive by November 30, 2008. He will have gathered and delivered any requested information to the customers with 100 percent accuracy within three days of their requests.

Goal 3: Joe will complete a training program for the online order processing system and correctly process fifteen sample orders using the system.

Goals for 4–6 Months of Employment

Goal 4: Joe will process all purchase orders using the correct procedure and confirm orders with each customer within two days of their receipt.

Goal 5: Joe will maintain at least 90 percent of the sales level from the fourth quarter of 2007 during the fourth quarter of 2008.

Goals for 7–9 Months of Employment

Goal 6: Joe will complete all purchase orders with 100 percent accuracy within twenty-four hours of receipt using the online system.

Goal 7: Joe will meet the sales level of the first quarter of the previous year in the first quarter of 2009.

Goal 8: Joe will develop at least three new customers and have received at least one order from each by the end of the ninth month.

Note that Joe was given a sufficient period of time to learn the product, the order processing system, and the current customers.

During the next three months, he was given a sales goal lower than the level of the previous experienced salesperson during the year before. Finally, by his third quarter of employment, he was expected to meet the previous salesperson's sales level and to begin developing new customers. The numbers used to set the goals should be taken from the previous job holder's performance during the year before he started. In the future, Joe will be expected to increase sales and to develop new customers continuously. His goals will increase as he proves himself capable of doing the work and rising to the challenge. What if he had missed a goal during the first or third quarters? Then the manager needs to rethink the goal. If the manager believes that the goal was challenging, it can be extended for another quarter. If the manager believes that the goal was easily achievable, then Joe's ability to perform at the necessary level and his future with the organization must be considered.

Many managers intuitively believe that subordinates should be involved in goal setting. It makes sense that when people have a say in setting their own performance level, they will be committed to it. That is not necessarily true. The research on "participatively set" goals is mixed. Sometimes, people do better if they have a say in setting their own goals and other times, they do not. Most of the time, it is acceptable for the manager to set the goals and explain them to the worker. One exception is that it helps to involve the worker in determining the goal if the task is complex and if the worker must use his or her specific expertise (e.g., when working with professionals) to find a way to complete it. For example, if the engineer who designed a piece of equipment is working on the marketing strategy, let her set the timeline for completion of the drawings that will be used in the product Web site.

BARRIERS TO ACHIEVING GOALS

Occasionally, goal conflict can occur. The previous example of the medical transcriptionists is an example. Accuracy and quantity of work were the major priorities and customer service interfered with those. Another example would be the nurse whose goals include limiting patient complaints *and* serving increasing numbers of patients on his floor. The nurse may have trouble meeting both goals. It is the manager's responsibility to know what the breaking point is—how many patients can an experienced nurse care for effectively? Then, the head nurse has to negotiate with senior managers in the hospital for the appropriate staffing levels. If workers are asked to do the impossible, they will become frustrated and irrational and unpredictable behavior results or the nurse will leave.

Another problem with goal attainment can occur when organizational barriers make work more difficult. For example, if specific software is necessary to complete a project design, but the organization will not approve the purchase of it until the next budget cycle, the goal may not be met. If an individual must answer constantly ringing phones while trying to concentrate on a detailed task, there will be problems. An effective manager runs interference for the rest of the team, removing barriers, providing necessary supplies, and negotiating with other departments.

A common problem with goal setting occurs if the compensation system in a company rewards only those who fully accomplish their individual goals. As mentioned earlier, challenging goals lead to higher levels of performance and should not be met every year. If they are, they probably were not challenging. So, this means that people who have the most challenging goals will not be rewarded. Obviously, this is a problem. There are a couple of strategies for overcoming this issue, but each one has its own strengths and weaknesses.[1] Here are two.

1. Employees can be paid rewards based on the percentage of increased levels of performance over the previous year. For example, if one reduced customer complaints of twenty-eight last year by 10 percent (three less), she would receive a bonus of 1 percent; by 25 percent (seven less), the bonus would be 2 percent, or by 50 percent (fourteen less), a 3 percent bonus would be earned. Obviously, these figures would have to be determined by those with knowledge of the job based on the dollar value to the organization. If complaints result in $50 lower sales or $5 lower profits, the bonus would not have to

be as high as they would if complaints led to $100,000 losses in business.

2. Managers make decisions about the rewards at the end of the performance period. This way, managers would have flexibility to decide what the performance was worth after the fact. They could take into account all of the variables that occurred that would have affected the process. This leaves the decision open to accusations of bias, naturally, but if managers are well trained and effective, you should be able to trust their judgment.

So far, we have talked primarily about individual goals. However, goals can and should be established for each department and each unit within the department before individual goals can be set. For example, if a CEO has made eliminating levels of bureaucracy part of his vision, the manager of each department should set a goal for the department which is consistent with that vision. Departmental goals should also be challenging and specific. This departmental goal will then provide guidance as to what managers and supervisors should be leading their staffs to accomplish.

WRITING GOALS

Writing goals is not difficult, but it involves taking apart the process of achieving the organizational vision. Starting with the vision, the CEO (or whatever the key leader of the organization is called) must meet with each executive in the organization individually. She must explain her vision for the organization and the role that each department will play in achieving the vision. The two must outline what must be done in that department very specifically. In addition, the CEO will tell the executive for what he will be held accountable—typically this will be the departmental goals themselves, but the executive may also be given some personal developmental goals as well. These goals must be very specific— exactly what will be done, what conditions apply, and what time frame is required? We prefer to begin the written goal statement with an action verb. In the case of a personal development goal, it might read, "The XYZ manager will successfully complete the ABC training program by March 31, 2008."

Then, the executive takes the departmental goals to those who report to him and the process begins over. This goes down the reporting line. Production workers are more apt to have production goals which should be met, but whenever possible, everyone should be involved in implementing change. In other words, if an organization is trying to improve efficiency, production workers and janitors usually have very good ideas and should be asked to develop suggestions based on their experience. In addition, this is part of strategic planning. By top-down goal setting, the organization has direction. It is going somewhere that it has chosen to go.

Here are examples of goals for various positions based on pieces of particular organizational visions and related departmental goals. These are provided in order to show how goals should be written and how they should relate to the vision by way of departmental goals, but only the managers can establish the actual level of performance necessary to make the goals challenging and specific in any one situation. Note the wording, the specificity, and the measurability of the goals.

Organizational Type: *Fortune* 100 Multinational Corporation

Vision Includes: Eliminating Bureaucracy.

Goal for the Marketing Department:

Every decision-making process in the department will be documented. At least one level of the process will be cut for each within the year, which will shorten all decision making by at least two weeks.

Goal for a Marketing Director:

Levels of approval for all print ads will be cut by at least one level and the process will be shortened by one week.

Goal for the Operations Department:

The supply purchasing process will be completely revised to eliminate all intermediaries between the unit supervisor who places the order and the purchasing manager who finds the supplier and makes the purchase within one year.

Goal for an Operations Manager:

Purchasing will be decentralized to each department and included in a revised purchasing report provided monthly to the executive staff with variations noted.

Goal for a Production Worker:

At least two suggestions for cost cutting on the production floor will be given directly to the operations manager during the year.

Goal for the Facilities Management Department:

Within three months, the purchasing department will be moved closer to the department which does most of the ordering.

Goal for an Administrative Assistant in Facilities Management:

By the end of the year, all facility records including square footage and office configurations will be transferred to electronic files with full accessibility by all employees.

Organizational Type: Advertising Agency

Vision Includes: Increasing Business in the Soft Drink Industry to 25 Percent of Overall Revenue.

Goal for the Marketing Department:

The department will develop a comprehensive strategy to increase business in the soft drink business and obtain approval from senior management within nine months.

Goal for a Marketing Director:

Identify, contact, and develop marketing proposals for at least two of the largest soft drink companies at the end of an advertising cycle by the end of the year. The proposals will include a list of services that could be provided, 3–4 ideas for a revised approach, projected service delivery dates for the following year, samples of work for similar organizations, and descriptions of the staff.

Goal for the Operations Department:

Prepare for increased business within the year and be ready to handle a 25 percent increase in the work load in terms of both personnel and necessary equipment and software.

Goal for an Operations Manager:

Investigate the types of advertising done for the industry and hire the staff and purchase the equipment necessary to meet the projected needs.

Goal for a Technical Worker in the Marketing Department:

Draft 3–4 unique ideas for advertising of diet beverages including print ads, Web site advertising, and billboards with chips that read license plates.

Goal for the Facilities Management Department:

Find, design, and prepare space for a new unit to handle a new market segment within one block of the main office by the end of the year.

Goal for an Administrative Assistant in Facilities Management:

Contact the staff in operations who will need space and obtain their facility specifications. This will be transcribed and delivered to the manager of the department by the end of the second quarter.

Organizational Type: Small Plastics Manufacturing Company

Vision Includes: Better Cost Management.

Goal for the Marketing Department:

Complete a cost analysis for the marketing department by the end of the first quarter with a plan to reduce costs by 5 percent without sacrificing quality.

Goal for a Marketing Director:

Evaluate all current methods and staff involved in product marketing with an extensive analysis and rationale for current marketing costs. A plan for a 10 percent reduction should be included.

Goal for the Operations Department:

Complete a cost analysis for the department by the end of the first quarter with a plan to reduce costs by 5 percent without losing quality.

Goal for an Operations Manager:

Evaluate all current operations costs and develop a cost analysis which identifies opportunities to reduce operations costs by 10 percent.

Goal for a Production Worker:

Identify at least two sources of waste in the production area within the first six months of the year.

Goal for the Facilities Management Department:

Complete a cost analysis for the department by the end of the first quarter with a plan to reduce costs by 5 percent without losing quality.

Goal for an Administrative Assistant in Facilities Management:

Track and identify all superfluous written communications within the department, report those to the supervisors, and immediately reduce all communication redundancy.

Organizational Type: Large Dairy Agribusiness

Vision Includes: Increased Efficiency.

Goal for the Marketing Department:

Examine and report on all developing markets within the industry with a complete analysis of the impact on efficiency.

Goal for a Marketing Director:

Identify the developing markets in dairy like organic, nonantibiotic fed cows, PETA-approved operations, etc., and submit a full report by the end of the first quarter.

Goal for the Operations Department:

Examine and report on all current practices within the department with a complete analysis of efficiency improvements which could be implemented within the year.

Goal for an Operations Manager:

Identify and test all new dairy equipment introduced since current equipment was purchased and submit an analysis of efficiency improvements which can be projected with their purchase.

Goal for a Production Worker:

Record all steps taken for every dairy production process for one week and submit the completed form at the end of the month.

Goal for the Facilities Management Department:

Prepare a complete analysis of all current space use both on the administrative and farm side and include proposals to control costs by consolidating facilities usage where possible by the end of the third quarter.

Goal for an Administrative Assistant in Facilities Management:

Develop and distribute tracking forms for the production workers. Tabulate the results into an EXCEL report for every departmental manager by the end of the second quarter.

These examples give you an idea of how vision and goals fit together. Note that you have been given only a piece of each organization's vision. In addition, note that goals develop from the top down. It is impossible for executives to achieve their visions and departmental goals if the goals in the units and for the employees under them are not consistent.

This is a strenuous process. Too often managers get discouraged or bored with it and give up. When the goals are written, monitored and achieved, organizational visions are more likely to be fulfilled. Like every aspect of management, doing it right is hard work and requires the drive to get it right.

NOTES

1. E. A. Locke, "Linking goals to monetary incentives," *Academy of Management Executive* 18 (2004): 22–25.

FOUR

Creating and Modeling
an Ethical Environment

WorldCom. Tyco. HealthSouth. Adelphia. Boeing. Enron. You have no doubt heard the litany of these and other companies that have been in the news for all of the wrong reasons since the start of the new millennium. A number of their former leaders represent notorious poster children for unethical misdeeds, and just plain illegal behavior in the name of doing business. Consider these individuals who until very recently were celebrated by many in the business media for their achievements and success:

- Bernie Ebbers—former CEO of the telecommunications company WorldCom, currently serving a twenty-five-year prison sentence for fraud and conspiracy.
- Dennis Kozlowski—former CEO of the conglomerate Tyco International, currently serving an eight-year-plus prison sentence for misappropriation of funds.
- Richard Scrushy—founder of the health care company Health-South, currently serving a prison sentence after his conviction for bribery, mail fraud, and obstruction of justice.
- John Rigas—cofounder of Adelphia Communications Corporation, at its peak one of the largest cable companies in the

United States, currently serving a prison sentence after his conviction on multiple counts of bank, wire, and securities fraud. Together with two of his sons and other former business associates, Mr. Rigas essentially looted Adelphia to the tune of billions of dollars, which ultimately led to its filing for bankruptcy.

- Executives and high-level employees at The Boeing Company—a recent series of ethical breeches at one of the world's most admired aerospace and defense companies including charges by the Justice Department of violation of industrial espionage laws.

- The men of Enron Corporation—Kenneth Lay (deceased, former Chairman and CEO), Jeffrey Skilling (former CEO and chief operating officer), Andrew Fastow (former CFO), and a handful of other erstwhile executives of the onetime energy giant, convicted for securities fraud and related crimes, or parties to myriad plea agreements and other legal maneuvers. If these fellows truly represented "the smartest guys in the room," as they were called in the eponymous book and movie documentary of the Enron debacle, then we would surely hope to avoid meeting the others. The Enron fiasco created all sorts of collateral damage, including illumination of the accounting scandal that ultimately took down Arthur Andersen LLP, formerly one of the "Big Five" accounting firms, which was involved lock-step in perpetrating the fraud. Its involvement provided the impetus for the federal legislation aimed at reforming public accounting and protecting investors known as the Sarbanes-Oxley Act of 2002.

The list of recent high-profile ethical transgressions is most certainly not limited to business. Political figures including former U.S. representatives Gary Condit, Randy "Duke" Cunningham, Tom DeLay, Mark Foley, Newt Gingrich, Bob Livingston, Bob Ney, current U.S. representative William Jefferson, and U.S. senators Larry Craig and David Vitter form a "who's who" roster of disgraced congressional power brokers. Jack Abramoff, political lobbyist and convicted felon, was associated with several of the aforementioned congressmen.

For good measure, let us not fail to mention the world of sports, where Atlanta Falcons quarterback Michael Vick is awaiting sentencing after pleading guilty to several charges incident to his dog fighting enterprise, celebrated New England Patriots Head Coach Bill Belichick was punished by the National Football League for cheating by videotaping opponents' signals in direct violation of league rules (despite his statement that he only misinterpreted league rules), and the world's most prestigious bicycle racing event, the Tour of France, has become an annual Tour de Farce infested by allegations of blood doping and the use of performance enhancing drugs on the part of its contestants.

NASA astronauts, Olympic athletes, baseball sluggers, at least one former National Basketball Association official, and a host of others have also been caught up in ethically questionable situations. What is going on? Why are so many people in positions of high regard and lofty expectations parading by on television doing the "perp walk" in orange jumpsuits, shuffling into court surrounded by teams of lawyers, or standing in front of a bank of microphones issuing apologies or other expressions of contrition as their families stand beside them, smiling thinly in their unflagging support? Is this an epidemic, or are we just becoming more aggressive about discovering instances of ethical lapses and publicizing them as lurid entertainment to alleviate our boredom? The fact is that we do not usually read or hear about good ethical behavior because it seldom makes for news. Nor are we often aware of the myriad small ethical lapses that happen in organizations everyday. Headlines focus on major ethical lapses that have severe consequences, such as those mentioned above.

When does behavior cross the line from questionable to smarmy to unethical to illegal? That is a fair question, and one that many managers should be asking themselves. Ethical meltdowns threaten organizations as surely as poor planning, lousy customer service, inept leadership, and careless accounting. So what should managers do? You might assume that ethics is just the concern of executives, but the examples cited above reveal that egregious ethical flaws can occur at the top even if most employees are doing their best to behave in an ethical manner. And although you might not think that there is much that is within your power to influence, you would be mistaken. Research suggests, and practice bears out, that middle- and lower-level managers have significantly more influence on the ethical behavior of their employees than executives and top-level managers. Accordingly, you should take this aspect of your job very seriously. You can do plenty.

CREATING AN ETHICAL WORKPLACE

To create an ethical working environment, we should first understand what is meant by ethics. The word ethics is derived from the Greek word *ethos,* which means the customs or characteristics that apply to a person, a people, or an institution. For our purposes, ethics are a system of rules, standards, principles, or values that guide the conduct of a person or govern members of a profession, especially with respect to what is acceptable or unacceptable. That definition is a bit of a mouthful, but it is also pretty vague, allowing for a lot of latitude concerning what constitutes right and wrong. Intellectually, the domain of ethics bridges the domains of free choice and law. Most of us would agree that there are problems associated with trying to operate a society under conditions of free choice, and that we need to define some standards to prevent chaos. But at the same time we would also concur that all of our standards cannot, or should not, be defined or dictated by laws, because that would be enormously complex and nothing would ever get accomplished. Ethics, therefore, are useful social standards that vary from setting to setting.

One thing that you must keep in mind is that although the existence of formal ethical mechanisms and structures in organizations can have some positive impact on the ethical behavior of employees, those mechanisms and structures by themselves are very unlikely to create an ethical work environment. Formal ethical mechanisms and structures include written codes of conduct, ethics training, ethics ombudsmen, "hotlines" for reporting ethics violations in confidence or anonymously, and the like. They might serve to set the tone, but there are several problems associated with them in practice that severely limit their effectiveness.

First, most employees are introduced to them exactly once— during their orientation after they have joined an organization.

During that time, they are swamped with information, including the insurance options they should consider, what pension plan to sign up for, how to get a parking permit, meeting coworkers, etc. Ethics information tends to get tossed in with a myriad of other "boiler plate H.R. stuff"—you know, work place civility, affirmative action, antidiscrimination, employee rights and responsibilities, and other topics—so it loses much of the impact that it might otherwise have. Further, without any reinforcement, employees conclude (quite logically, in fact) that ethics is not very high on management's list of priorities. They figure that they will do the right thing and assume that most of their coworkers will do so too.

Second, if they are not reinforced, those mechanisms and structures will take on the appearance of window dressing and not elicit much seriousness. Everybody has heard of organizations that espouse explicit ethical standards and principles, and yet somehow still manage to make splashy headlines for ethical misdeeds. Enron, for example, had an ethics code, as did Boeing. Both companies pointed to theirs with pride prior to their problems becoming public. Ironically, Arthur Andersen, who headed the firm with his name on the letterhead for years, was a paragon of ethics in accounting, where he was a major force in establishing high standards in the industry. His reputation for honesty arose from his refusal to take on lucrative work that wasn't strictly above board, and his motto was "think straight, talk straight," which flowed down through his company and provided the foundation for years of growth and prosperity.

Third, if employees witness behavior that conflicts with those mechanisms and structures, yet goes unpunished or is rewarded, they become confused and quickly become skeptical about a lot more than just ethics. There is nothing quite as powerful as insincerity or, worse, hypocrisy among the higher-ups to make you check your own values at the door. Culture, values, and norms that are espoused and that develop informally must be consistent with each other to shape the behavior of individuals in a productive direction; incongruity leads to dysfunction.

Fourth, ethical mechanisms and structures that exist in many organizations are simply inadequate for guiding people through ethical dilemmas, or situations that arise when they have to choose from among alternatives that all present potentially negative consequences. By their very nature, such decisions are complex, multifaceted problems with significant situational and personal dimensions. For example, if you were a project manager for a large U.S. construction company, and you had a multimillion dollar contract to build a school in a foreign country whose culture required bribing officials to get their approval at every point along the way, what would you do? On the one hand, you could go along and play the game, complete the contract even though you violate U.S. law, and hope that you and your company never have to face the consequences that would accrue if that information was made public. On the other hand, you could refuse to play the game, lose the contract, be required to lay off your work force, deprive the children of that region of a well-needed school, and perhaps lose your job as well, but maintain your principles and values. Tough decision, isn't it? The good news is that very few of our ethical decisions involve stakes that high with so much ambiguity.

ETHICAL BEHAVIOR TRUMPS LEGAL BEHAVIOR

Unfortunately, it isn't enough to simply behave legally. Of course managers have legal responsibilities, but most of the time those responsibilities barely scratch the surface of ethical obligation. Adhering to the law is near the bottom of the ethical pyramid, so to speak. Doing what is legal is not the same as doing what is right, and if you train your employees to only behave legally and reward them accordingly, that is what they will do. If your organization functions that way, you should not be surprised by instances of ethical lapses. Acting within the confines of the law is the bare minimum that might keep you out of the news, but it can also have negative repercussions. Do not assume that if something is legal it must be acceptable.

Consider the disaster that occurred at the Union Carbide subsidiary pesticide plant in Bhopal, India, in 1984. Cited as one of the worst industrial disasters in history, the plant accidentally released tons of toxic gas which immediately killed 3,000 people in the surrounding area and ultimately caused approximately 20,000 deaths. Investigations conducted in the aftermath of the disaster revealed that the company's cost-cutting measures were largely to blame—moving the plant to a less-densely populated area was considered too expensive, quality control had become less stringent, safety rules had been relaxed, and the plant was being operated by fewer qualified operators to reduce labor costs, among other factors. Union Carbide defended its practices, claiming that the plant had been sabotaged and that in any event the plant satisfied local legal operating requirements. After the tragedy, the company agreed to compensate injured survivors and the families of the deceased. The sad legacy of that disaster was that it could have been avoided. Legal obligations? Satisfied—*check*! Ethical responsibilities? You be the judge. Unfortunately, we have witnessed that same pattern on too many occasions—first stonewall, then accept no fault, then shift the blame, then admit to minor errors when cornered, then do only what is legally required, then cut your losses, and finally write a check after reaching a financial settlement well after the fact.

Research suggests that programs and practices focused on promoting good ethical behavior are more effective than those that are aimed at ensuring compliance with laws and regulations, and that hybrid programs that both require employees to obey the law and encourage them to go above and beyond the law are the most effective of all. Encourage your employees to aspire to do the right thing, and they will come through for you far more often than they will fail.

EFFECTIVE ETHICAL MECHANISM AND STRUCTURES

To create an ethical work place, ethical mechanisms must be established. But understand that they are a necessary but not sufficient condition for ethics to flourish. Here are some mechanisms that have proven to be effective:

Screen prospective employees. Your first line of defense against unethical behavior is to employ people who possess a history of ethical behavior and values consistent with high ethical standards.

Paper-and-pencil honesty tests are one means of screening, and they are generally valid if administered and analyzed by experts. One of us knows of an academic colleague who was administered such a test by a university, with its scoring and analysis left in the hands of the department to which he was applying. That is a bad idea. Knowing whether he admitted to ever having permanently borrowed a pen from a previous employer hardly makes him a thief or a saint. Background investigations can be an extremely valuable tool for screening potential employees. The simplest background checks merely involve checking references (incidentally, nobody who will provide a reference will say anything bad about that person) and verifying transcripts—tasks that are seldom performed by most hiring organizations, believe it or not, even though it is common knowledge that up to half of all resumes and job applications contain at least one factual misstatement, deliberate or otherwise. More extensive background investigations can be expensive and time consuming, but might be essential when considering employees for high-level or sensitive positions.

Develop a meaningful code of ethical conduct. The key word here is "meaningful." Slogans or mottos such as "We do ethics right" won't do. A meaningful code of ethical conduct should clearly state your organization's basic ethical values, principles, and expectations, as well as consequences for violations. It should also discuss foreseeable potential ethical dilemmas which may be faced by your employees and prescribe what actions are to be taken in those instances. It must be communicated to everybody, but it is important that it be communicated in an open forum with as much participation as possible. In other words, don't expect people to accept it at face value and blindly obey its every nuance. Instead, share it, talk about it, and help your people internalize it. In that way they will be most likely to accept it.

Provide ongoing ethics training. Creating an ethical work place is a process, not a onetime or periodic event. Although your employees' first exposure to your organization's ethical principles will probably occur during their orientation, you need to make sure that you revisit those principles at every opportunity. Initial training will decay if it is not refreshed. Discussion of ethical lapses at other companies as they are reported is valuable. Just read *Business Week;* you will have plenty of fodder. Alternatively, discuss real or fictitious cases or scenarios, and help people develop mechanisms that they should use if similar situations occur on the job. Solicit people's experiences with ethical dilemmas in the past and use them as opportunities for experiential learning.

Establish appropriate structures. Structures include positions such as an ethical ombudsman to receive reports of ethical violations. That person should have sufficient seniority to get investigations started, and should have the ear of top managers. Accordingly, a clear line of communication right to the top is necessary and employees need to know that it exists. An ethics "hotline" might also be valuable because it ensures anonymity of the reporting party. Whatever way you decide to handle it, you must ensure that those structures do not become empty drop boxes for employee complaints. They should serve a valuable function by providing critical information to management that might signal potential problems that require action. It usually takes a lot to get people to report on one another, so if they do, you can take it for granted that something really big might be ready to blow up in your face. Make certain that those structures are set up to provide feedback to the reporter.

Reinforce ethical behavior. It is absolutely critical that both ethical and unethical behavior is recognized in a timely and appropriate manner. Your employees should be rewarded openly for behaving ethically, particularly when behaving unethically might have been the path of least resistance. That will help insure that they will behave similarly in the future, as well as spill over to others who see that ethical behavior is not only expected, but appreciated and recognized.

Punish unethical behavior. Punishing employees is something that most managers find difficult to do, particularly if they have developed a close working relationship with that person, and there are of course many restrictions and factors that play into how much you can reveal to others regarding the punishment. However, you are paid to make the tough calls. After you have punished the offender, you should let it be known to others that certain types of behavior will not be tolerated. Many managers use the informal communication network, or the "grapevine," to spread this news, but we believe that is too haphazard. Have a meeting, discuss the inappropriate behavior openly, and establish a dialog with your people so that it becomes an opportunity for learning.

Organizations that establish effective structures and mechanisms enjoy a side benefit that is extremely valuable: they are able to use ethics as a recruiting and retention tool to get and keep the right kind of employees. Ethics can then be used for managerial development, which results in sustaining the organization's commitment to ethics—a self-reinforcing process that serves to guard against ethical lapses.

MODELING AN ETHICAL WORK PLACE

At this point, you must be aware that we have made several assumptions: (1) that *you* are going to behave ethically, (2) that you cannot do much about the ethical behavior of those above you in your organization's hierarchy, and (3) that your real concern is about the ethical behavior of your employees. Your employees' decisions to behave ethically or unethically are influenced by a number of factors, some of which are individual and some of which are organizational. Frankly, you don't have much control over those individual factors, once those people are hired and/or assigned to you. However, as their immediate supervisor, you can exert tremendous influence over those organizational factors; in fact, far more than you might ever imagine. We know that you can be far more effective in communicating the value of ethical behavior to employees than even the most articulate and well-crafted written statement of ethical philosophy could possibly be.

Modeling an ethical work place is a powerful leadership technique that you can use to enhance your overall effectiveness as a manager. Does that sound too good to be true? Trust us, it works. Modeling essentially comes down to showing your employees, through your own words and actions, how you want them to behave. The fact of the matter is that people need, expect, and appreciate ethical guidance from their leaders—and that means you.

When your employees perceive you to be an ethical person, they feel more valued as contributors to the organization, are more satisfied with their jobs and the organization in general, and will be far more likely to behave ethically themselves. Those factors in turn make it easier for you to lead, and ethical leaders have been shown to be more effective leaders—powerful stuff indeed! To reiterate what we said earlier, you have far more influence on your subordinates than anybody else in your organization, so use that influence wisely.

The modeling process begins with an honest and thorough self-examination. First and foremost, you must be an ethical role model. Regardless of your wishes, how you feel about your inadequacies as a leader, and for better or worse, you are the most salient role model for your employees. We have all heard the famous athletes who proclaim "I am not a role model," but whether they like it or not, they are, even if they behave like idiots. Kids aspire to be like them—they have ability, money, and fame (or notoriety). So do rock stars and rappers. So do politicians and painters. So do you, albeit in a far more circumscribed sense. Anyway, the bottom line is that in your position, the ethical behavior of your employees is your responsibility, so use your status as a role model to your advantage.

Become an ethical leader. What do ethical leaders do? Well, it is too simple to state that they lead by example. That much is obvious. Others' perceptions of you are influenced greatly by your values, and those perceptions will feature prominently in their own decision making and actions. If you tell others to do as you say and not as you do, it's all over. People will lose whatever respect they had for you and you don't have a chance to exert anything remotely close to ethical leadership. Accordingly, the first thing that you must do is set an example. That certainly applies to your behavior at work, but it also carries over to your behavior in your personal life. How you live your own life, both professionally **and** personally, is critical to others' perceptions of you as an ethical leader. That might not seem fair to you, but fairness has nothing to do with it. If people learn of ethical inconsistencies in their leaders, they become callous and many will start to feel that they, too, can behave unethically. You must walk the talk, as they say. Your personal integrity is only the beginning—a necessary but not sufficient condition, as we are fond of saying. First, you must decide what is right—usually pretty easy unless you are of questionable character to begin with. Then you must *do* what is right —which is much more difficult because of all of the pressures that you confront (e.g., make the numbers, keep your people employed, handle peer pressure to fit in, "get with the program," etc.). If you succeed in doing what is right, you will earn respect that enables you to multiply your effectiveness as a leader.

Be guided by your own convictions, and understand that those convictions will establish the foundation for your overall effectiveness as a leader. Some research suggests that ethical leadership is associated with a number of positive outcomes—and no research of which we are aware suggests that ethical leadership is associated with any negative outcomes, or that unethical leadership is associated with any positive outcomes. Therefore, even if you are *still* skeptical about the power of ethics, pay heed to the old adage about chicken soup: it might not make you well but it sure doesn't do you any harm.

Trust is essential to modeling an ethical environment. Employees want to trust their leaders, and trust makes it much easier for you to accomplish things with and through people—the essence of leadership. Leaders who have earned the trust of their followers are allowed more discretion and can make the occasional error without losing their effectiveness. How do you develop trust? Honesty, open communication, doing what you say you will do, and getting to know your employees as people are usually the key. There is evidence that trust is the most important trait in all relationships whether they are personal or professional.

After you have established your ethical leadership, show people the way. This takes constant work, because modeling ethical behavior is a *process*, not an event:

- Lead them along by making it acceptable to talk about ethics.
- Take time—or make time—during regular meetings to commend somebody who has demonstrated ethical conduct or pointed out a potentially questionable ethical situation for correction.

- Include dimensions of ethical behavior on your employees' annual performance evaluations to emphasize its importance.
- Talk about the benefits of ethical behavior as often as you can in informal sessions.
- Encourage your people to see you if they have any questions or concerns about the actions of your work unit.
- Communicate, communicate, communicate—open lines of communication have numerous benefits, and when people want to speak about ethics you should drop whatever else you are doing and listen to what they have to say.
- Bring up historical examples of people in the organization who have gone above and beyond the call of duty to accomplish some deed in an ethical manner instead of taking an available shortcut.
- Use your internal newsletter or bulletin to describe instances of ethical behavior and the benefits, as well as occasions of ethical lapses and their consequences.
- Reward instances of good ethical decision making and behavior whenever possible and with as much fanfare as you can.
- Do not allow rationalizations of unethical behavior. Every time one bad act is rationalized, the next one becomes easier. Remember the first time you cut a class in school? You probably felt guilty that first time. The second time you felt less guilt. The third time was easy. If you know that taking a tablet of paper from the office is wrong, do not excuse it the first time you or a colleague does it. If you do, then by the time one is taking computer equipment home, it has becomes easy. This is of course true for both personal and professional work behavior. Dishonesty escalates.

We would like to conclude this chapter with a few random thoughts about ethics.

If you have paid close attention, you will notice that we did not use the words "morals" and "morality" in our discussion. Morals are attributes formed by distinctly individual *attitudes*, and we chose instead to focus on *behaviors* that are evident and can be dealt with by managers.

Those who put themselves on ethical pedestals have the farthest to fall, and witnesses generally take delight as they plummet. Consider the pantheon of religious leaders who assail the decisions and ways of others, then get caught doing the same things. Few spectacles are more entertaining than watching hypocrites hoisted on their own petards, admitting to some sin or another only after they have been caught in the act, and then begging for forgiveness. We hope that you will not become one of them.

A few people who behave unethically and contrary to the values of their organization frequently do more damage to that organization and its reputation than a hundred people who act ethically can remedy. Although it might comfort us to believe that unethical behavior is usually the result of a few bad apples spoiling the whole barrel, we also know that where there is smoke, there is generally fire. Consider the example of the New Orleans Police Department officers who abandoned their city even before Hurricane Katrina came ashore. Although the majority of NOPD officers performed their jobs magnificently under essentially unbearable conditions, the number who did not represented such an unusual percentage of sworn officers that an investigation after the fact was conducted. That investigation revealed mismanagement, ineffective leadership, and ethical violations in the recruiting and hiring process for police officers. A rotting fish stinks from the head.

Ethics is a complex subject, and a good sense of what is right and what is wrong does not guarantee ethical behavior. Ethical decisions aren't made in a vacuum, and the context of each decision is an important determinant in how it is made. You can't control all of the factors, but you can influence some of the important ones. How your work unit acts and reacts ethically reveals a lot about you, for better or worse. Regardless, at the end of the day, you should be comfortable in the knowledge that you tried to establish an ethical climate for decision making and action. When all is said and done, organizations do not demonstrate ethical or unethical behavior—people do. The one thing that you absolutely never want to lose is your personal reputation for ethical behavior.

FIVE

Recruiting and Selecting the Best Employees

Hiring the best people to work for and with you is critical to success. It is the single most important task that a manager performs. Most managers faced with this responsibility have never been trained on how to recruit and select employees. Here is a step-by-step approach to hiring.

CREATE OR UPDATE THE JOB DESCRIPTION

The first step in hiring is to clearly outline KSAs (knowledge, skills, and abilities) necessary to do the job effectively. Most companies have formal job descriptions—in some cases legally mandated—that cover this information. But even if you have formal descriptions to draw on, make sure they are accurate.

Many managers make mistakes when it comes to identifying KSAs. Technical skills are fairly easy to identify. For example, if hiring an engineer, you would look for a candidate with an engineering degree from a reputable institution. However, if you think that all electrical engineers are the same, you have some unpleasant surprises in store for you. What are missing are the performance skills necessary for the type of work that you want done in your organization.

Let's get specific. The following list is not complete, but it will give you an idea of the difference between technical and performance skills. By the way, don't get hung up on putting the skills into the right category (i.e., technical vs. performance), just list every skill you are looking for in an engineer.

KSAs necessary for an electrical engineer in a consulting company

Technical skills	*Performance skills*
Appropriate analytical techniques for the specialty	Customer oriented
Testing procedures	Honest
Research skills for job	Multitasking ability
Mastery of engineering techniques	Good oral communication
	Selling skills

As mentioned, in most companies, job descriptions are written that summarize all of the tasks performed by an employee in each job. These descriptions help everyone understand exactly what is expected of them and they help the people doing the hiring identify the exact skills necessary to do the jobs effectively. A good job description includes the following information: (1) a brief summary statement describing the basic job responsibilities, (2) a list of any certifications, licenses, or degrees necessary, (3) a list of every task and responsibility that the job holder has, and (4) a list of any education and experience required to do the job. Using the job description, write a list of the technical and performance skills necessary for the position.

CREATE A POOL OF CANDIDATES

The second step in hiring is recruiting or creating a pool of qualified candidates. Many employers simply run an ad in the classified section of the Sunday newspaper (or the placement center of a professional organization) and hope that someone qualified applies. They also assume that the only candidates for their jobs are the ones who are looking for a job at that time. This is wrong.

The key to successful recruiting is to be proactive and aggressive. Don't settle for the candidates who find you through an ad or placement service. Here are some more recruiting strategies to consider:

1. *Ask your better employees/coworkers if they know anyone who is looking for a job.* Avoid relatives of employees. Ask them to think about employees in other organizations with whom they interact professionally. Is there anyone who is particularly helpful, intelligent, competent, or friendly? Of course, what you are seeking depends on the skills you have outlined. Call the recommended people and tell them about your job. Ask if they are interested in scheduling a phone interview to learn more. Referrals from trusted employees can be a gold mine.

2. *Look around you and ask other professionals.* If you need a receptionist, think about the people you have seen in action in the businesses you use. Maybe you are looking for an administrative assistant and your doctor has a billing clerk who is ready for a new challenge. How about that helpful pharmacy assistant in the drug store?

3. *Run job advertisements in professional journals.* Most professional organizations have placement services. With these types of ads you know that individuals who both have the right qualifications and are active in professional organizations are being recruited.

4. *Use employment agencies that specialize in the type of job you are filling.* Let the agencies do the work and screen applicants for you. However, talk to other managers in your field to find the best agencies which specialize in the types of employees you hire.

5. *Contact college placement services for jobs requiring undergraduate or master's degrees.* The colleges will do some of the basic screening for you—by major, GPA, and other relevant criteria.

6. *Consider running job ads outside the classified sections of newspapers.* A well-designed display advertisement in the financial section will attract potential applicants who are not on the market and read that section of the newspaper.

The number of qualified candidates you need will vary depending on the number of positions you must fill, the availability of people with the qualifications, and the job market. Generally, you should have three to five candidates who have the minimum technical qualifications for each opening.

Before you begin your search, develop a recruiting strategy in detail. Give specifics. Who are you going to contact? Where could job ads be placed? How will you hunt for qualified candidates? What will the recruiting cost be to the organization? Remember that you have lots of competition for good employees. If you do not get enough qualified applicants, keep looking and expand your recruiting strategy.

You must verify that each of the candidates has the appropriate certificates, licenses, degrees, etc. People lie about these things and they even manufacture fake diplomas. If a degree is necessary, check. A candidate's formal educational attainment, and specifically a college degree, is one of the easiest things for prospective employers to check, but they seldom do. All it takes is an official transcript. If a degree is not essential, don't ask about it. Online degrees are highly suspect. Many of them are not legitimate. You must do your homework to ensure that the finalists have the KSAs necessary to do the work.

Before beginning your selection process, contact the finalists and schedule a telephone interview. This will be a short (thirty minutes) conversation during which the job is explained and a realistic job preview is provided. That is, you tell each person about both the positive and negative aspects of the job (e.g., extensive travel). You should also provide the salary range, if possible, and let the candidate know if the salary is negotiable. Allow the candidate to ask questions about the organization and the job. Clear up questions you have about any confusing aspects of the application or resume. At the end of this discussion, ask the candidates if they are still interested in the job. If not, you will have saved both of you a great deal of time.

HIRE THE BEST

Assume that you have four candidates who appear to have the minimum technical qualifications for the job. Usually, we like to have at least three candidates at this stage so that you have more choice. This takes you to the next step. The third step in hiring the right people is through the selection process. Most employers do an unstructured employment interview and make their decisions based on subjective perceptions of that interview. We all like to think that we are good judges of character and, thereby, can predict who will be a good performer on the job. Unfortunately, most managers make many hiring mistakes and pay a price in terms of time and money later. There are much more effective tools for selection than an unstructured interview. But, they all take time and expertise which many managers do not have. In addition, to ensure the effectiveness and legality of your hiring practices, you must use the same selection tools with every candidate for a specific job.

Note: Title VII of the Civil Rights Act of 1964 provides assurance that all candidates regardless of race, ethnicity, religion, and gender will have equal opportunities for jobs. The *Uniform Guidelines on Employee Selection Procedures* used by the courts to evaluate hiring practices for the possibility of discriminatory practices insist that all candidates are treated the same.[1] For more on the laws regulating hiring and employment in general, visit www.eeoc.gov.

Here are some of the best selection tools.

1. *A structured interview based on job KSAs.* The next half of this chapter will provide a complete explanation of this tool. Research supports the use of structured interviews even when good cognitive ability tests are also used. This approach can be effectively used across jobs.

2. *Cognitive ability testing.* These tests can determine general ability (basic intelligence—a good predictor of performance across jobs), mechanical ability, verbal ability, mathematical ability, etc. A good testing service can help you match a job's KSA with validated and reliable tests. Research tells us that cognitive ability tests are the most effective selection tools. General ability has been shown to predict job performance across all types of jobs. However, not all tests are necessary for all jobs. For example, a mechanical ability test would be very useful

when hiring someone at the entry level for a maintenance job, but useless when hiring a data entry specialist.

3. *Personality testing.* Personality tests can help you identify the type of people who work well as part of a team, interact effectively with other people, handle stress well, have a strong motivation to be successful, etc. Again, a good testing service can help you identify the tests that effectively measure the desired KSAs.

    Despite their potential effectiveness, many organizations use personality tests ineffectively due to a lack of expertise. For example, one *Fortune* 500 company uses an old personality test which was tested for validity many years ago by correlating the various dimensions with actual job performance. (A correlation is a statistical score which infers a relationship between two scores.) That is a good way to establish the validity of a selection tool. However, this company now runs correlations between the old correlations (established over twenty years ago) and the scores earned by current applicants. The higher the resulting number, the more likely one will be hired. Unfortunately, this is an inappropriate statistical technique and leads to an invalid result. Due to the lack of expertise, they are wasting a potentially useful tool, using a great deal of time and money, and passing up qualified candidates for jobs.

4. *Honesty testing.* Paper and pencil tests can help you identify the candidates who are most likely to steal or commit fraud. Most large retailers have been using them for years. (By the way, lie detector tests cannot be used for selection, in general.) If you are filling a job where the employee would have access to valuable information and/or supplies, an honesty test could be very helpful. Work with an expert to find the right test.

    There are some ethical concerns about the use of honesty questionnaires. The reason is due to the design of psychometric tools (psychological measures). Honesty tests have items on them to measure "social desirability" or an individual's attempt to look better to others. For example, one item might ask test takers whether they "strongly agree," "agree," "neither agree nor disagree," "disagree," or "strongly disagree" with the following statement: "I have never thought about stealing anything from work." If a person responds by circling "Strongly disagree," the test assumes that the individual is lying. However, some people have suggested that it **is** possible that a person who has very strong moral values has never considered stealing anything. Currently, social desirability items assume that everyone has at least considered it.

5. *Work samples.* Look at samples of the candidates' previous work. For example, if you are hiring a marketing director, ask for a portfolio of promotional materials they have developed in previous jobs. The samples of work that you request should reflect the type of work that is actually performed in your organization and in the specific job. That is, if the individual would be responsible for developing informational brochures, request copies of previously developed informational brochures.

6. *Performance tests.* If you require all employees in your health center to know CPR, give them a dummy and ask for a demonstration. If the job is fixing televisions, provide a broken TV and ask the candidates to diagnose the problems and explain how it should be repaired.

   You must outline the "right answers" to the performance tests before giving them. For example, how do you want your employees to handle difficult customers? When you give a performance test where candidates role-play how they would handle a difficult customer, observe to see if they are using the approach that you consider to be the "right answer" for your organization. Evaluate each candidate using the same standard. Performance tests are a highly effective selection tool across jobs.

7. *Job applications.* Please note that most organizations use a common application for all jobs. If you are allowed by your Human Resources Department, use applications that gather only specific information about candidates' education and experience, relevant to your job and the job's selection KSAs. Be sure that every question is job related. (In other words,

don't ask about military experience unless that is a job requirement.) Create your own application form. This way, you can
tailor it for each job opening. The application should contain a
place for them to signify that the information they provide is
accurate. Some organizations even assign weights to specific
items and create a numerical score for each candidate based
on the application.

8. *References.* References from people who have been able to
observe the candidates' work and provide answers to specific
questions regarding technical expertise might be useful if you
are confident about the objectiveness and technical competence of the observer. Professors and other educators *should*
be honest, in general. However, personal references are absolutely terrible sources of information about performance
skills—they are not reliable or valid and they are totally
dependent on the individual providing the reference. Most
organizations will not give you information about past
employees except to verify dates of employment, job title,
and salary. Some managers do what they consider a "smart"
way to gather "the truth" about a candidate—they call a friend
who works or worked in the same organization and ask for
"inside information" without the candidate's permission. This
is totally inappropriate because it jeopardizes the individual's
current employment. And, once again, you may talk to the
only person who either likes or dislikes the applicant. The
information is useless.

9. *Drug Testing.* Most companies do this because "everybody else
is doing drug testing." That's not a bad reason if you are in an
industry where work accidents can occur. Use experts to conduct the testing, tell candidates early in the selection process
that the person who is offered the position will be tested, and
conduct the test after you have made your choice. Good tests
are expensive. If the job entails driving a busload of children,
construction of tall buildings, or security for a pharmaceutical
company, the cost is worth every penny.

10. *Physicals.* Physical and mental health exams should be done
only when there are job-related reasons to verify specific

aspects of health and fitness. The physical must be done after the job offer is made and must be done for every applicant who receives an offer. Hiring can be contingent on the passage of the physical. Again, it is best to use an expert—in most situations, this should be a physician who has an excellent understanding of the job for which the individual is being hired.

11. *Assessment Centers.* Research has shown that assessment centers can be useful for predicting management ability. The centers should be developed by experts and validated prior to their use for selection purposes. Typically, organizations use assessment centers to provide a controlled environment to help them collect information to enable them to evaluate and choose from among inside candidates for promotions.

12. *Bio-data.* Research suggests that certain bio-data (biographical information) can be a good predictor of job performance. For example, if your father was a salesman, you may be a better salesperson due to your early exposure to that aspect of business. However, only hiring sons and daughters of salespeople would be inappropriate. Gathering bio-data can result in obtaining personal information about candidates' lives and backgrounds that could lead to hiring biases. On the other hand, hiring people who had their own sales businesses as children (e.g., lemonade stands) may be legitimate and useful. The type of bio-data used must be validated. An expert could gather bio-data from current employees and attempt to find the childhood behaviors that best predict job performance. You could then use this type of information for selection purposes.

13. *Cloudy Mirror Test.* When some organizations have trouble finding good candidates for jobs, they sometimes use cloudy mirror tests—hold a mirror to the candidate's mouth and, if it clouds up, that person gets the job. They may also do this because they do not understand recruiting and selection strategies. Desperation and ignorance breed poor hiring practices. Poor hiring practices breed poor organizational performance and potentially dangerous work environments.

So which tool is best? That depends on what you need to know about the candidates. We recommend that managers use a combination of tools. Develop a selection strategy for each job. For example, if hiring a receptionist, it may be adequate to do the following:

1. A structured interview screening for the performance skills— done by the manager.
2. Personality test specifically examining attitudes toward other people and conscientiousness.
3. A performance test in which each candidate is asked to handle three to four "typical" phone calls.
4. A test on the software that will be used by the receptionist.

If hiring a marketing director, it may be appropriate to do the following:

1. A structured interview screening for the performance skills.
2. A work sample—a portfolio of promotional materials developed in a previous job.
3. A performance test that asks the candidate to consider a relevant marketing issue and to describe how it would be handled.

THE STRUCTURED INTERVIEW

The interview is the most widely used selection tool in the United States. When the interview is structured, it has high validity (i.e., it contributes to our ability to predict future work performance) and reliability (i.e., it gives us consistent information over time across candidates). A structured interview is a formal series of questions based on the technical and performance skills that are asked of all candidates and evaluated using a predetermined measure. Unfortunately, most business people use unstructured interviews. An unstructured employment interview is equivalent to a professor asking different students different exam questions unrelated to the material covered in the class. Unstructured interviews are not valid or reliable and often contain potentially illegal questions. They do not work. Developing a structured interview is time consuming, but becomes easier with practice and the same questions can be used each time the same position is filled. Here is how to do a structured interview.

1. Using the technical and performance skills identified before recruiting, the structured interview should be developed to gather information that will help select the best future work performer. Determine which skills can be best evaluated using an interview. Note that an interview is not the best way to determine whether someone can develop an engineering plan. An interview, however, can help you determine whether the candidate understands appropriate uses of specific engineering techniques. For each of the skills you identify, develop a set of two to four questions.

2. Use closed-ended questions—those requiring a yes or no, or factual, answer—to clear up any gaps in the work history, to identify names of past employers, to get the names of educational institutions, and to ask if the individual can deal with the working conditions. For example, (a) "Your application says that you worked for Dr. Scott. What type of research does Dr. Scott do?" (b) "I noticed that you have a 5 year gap in your employment history. Where were you employed during that time?" (c) "This job would require you to be on your feet most of the work day. Would that be a problem for you?" Ask only as many questions as necessary to gather the information that you need.

3. Use open-ended behavioral and situational interview questions—those requiring more than a simple yes/no or factual answer—to clarify less tangible performance skills. Ask at least one of each and preferably a third question. You are trying to get at a behavioral pattern. If you ask only one question for each skill, you may get the wrong answer. Two more questions may reveal different information about the applicant. Since people are typically nervous during an employment interview, the first answer may have been related to stress rather than an

accurate picture of the candidate's skills. You are looking for patterns.

4. Behavioral interview questions have been empirically tested and produce valid results. These questions ask a candidate to reflect and share past experiences and work performance. The candidate tells you how she has performed in the past—a pretty good indication of how she will behave when working for you. Here are some examples. Note (a) the skill being evaluated and (b) the italicized phrases in each question.

   Customer orientation: *"Describe a time when you* had to give a client bad news. *Tell me how you did it."*

   Ability to take initiative: *"Tell me about a situation when* a problem occurred with a customer's bill and your supervisor was not around. *What did you do?"*

   Ability to work with others: *"Describe a situation in your current job when* you had to get information for a coworker from a number of people. *How did you* get the information you needed on a timely basis?"

   Ability to handle stress: *"Think of a time* when you had a difficult situation occur with a project. *Tell me about it. What did you do* to alleviate the stress?"

   Ability to solve equipment problems: *"Explain a situation in your current job when* a piece of equipment broke on a busy work day. *What did you do?"*

5. Situational interview questions have been empirically tested and produce valid results. These questions ask a candidate to speculate on how he/she would deal with a hypothetical situation. The situations used for these questions should be real situations that have occurred in the past in your organization. People tend to accurately predict how they will perform and you can decide if that is what you want. Here are some examples. Note the italicized wording.

   Customer orientation: *"Imagine that you are* serving food and a customer spits out the food and begins swearing. *What would you do?"*

   Ability to take initiative: *"Suppose that* the manager is gone for the day and cannot be reached. A customer calls to say that he must talk to the manager immediately. *What would you do?"*

Ability to work with others: *"If you were* assigned to work with an administrative assistant whom you disliked, *what would you do?"*

Ability to handle stress: *"If you had* a very stressful morning before arriving at the office, *what would you do* to prepare yourself to deal with problems?"

Ability to solve equipment problems: *"Pretend that* the overhead projector broke during an important presentation. *What would you do?"*

6. Review your questions to make sure they are job related. Throw out any that are not. If the information you are gathering is not job related, answers to the question might give you reasons to discriminate against a good candidate or in favor of a bad candidate.

Do not ask personal questions about the candidates unless a question is specifically job related. This is called BFOQ (Bona Fide Occupational Qualification). For example, if you need a Spanish speaker to work with bilingual customers, you may ask candidates if they speak Spanish. You should not ask if the candidates learned to speak Spanish from their parents. What if the hospital is Catholic? No, you cannot ask if the candidates are Catholic unless, for example, you are hiring a priest to counsel Catholic patients and their families. Then, that may be a legitimate job qualification. The skill or qualification must be job related or you may find yourself involved in a lawsuit.

Don't ask about owning a car, having children, or marriage. Many people **incorrectly** assume that car owners are less likely to be late for work, that mothers miss more work than nonmothers, and that married men are more responsible at work than single men. Don't ask and you won't have to deal with your own biases (or with a discrimination lawsuit later).

When a candidate tells you more than you need to know, set it aside cognitively. That is, think about it and let it go. For example, if a candidate tells you that he is a recovering alcoholic, legally you cannot discriminate against him. If a candidate tells you that she is pregnant, legally you cannot discriminate against her. Either revelation may cause you some concern about a candidate, but, legally, you cannot use the information to make a decision. You must set it aside when you make the decision.

7. Determine the "right answer" to each question. You must know what you are looking for or you won't find it. For example, if you asked candidates how they have handled difficult customers in their current job, the right answer depends on what you need in the position you are filling. If you want a nurse who is patient and handles difficult patients gently, "I stopped, carefully explained what I was doing and why, and waited until he was calm," would be the right answer. If you want a bouncer who deals aggressively with customers involved in an argument, "I gave him one warning and when he started yelling again, I escorted him to the exit," would be the right answer.

   The right answer is the yardstick by which you measure all candidates. Keep in mind that an interviewee may educate *you* about a good answer, but remember to give credit to other candidates for that answer as well.

8. After the initial screening, you should be interviewing three to five finalists who have the basic technical qualifications. Look over each candidate's application and resume or vita (a resume is an advertisement—take it with a grain of salt) and tailor the questions to each individual. The questions will remain basically the same, but instead of saying, "Tell me about a time when you were working at your current job and...," you will say, "Tell me about a time when you were working at K-Mart and..."

9. If a candidate recently graduated from school, that person may not have significant work experience. A question regarding interpersonal skills may sound like this, "Think of a time when you were working on a school project and a fellow student did not complete his part of the project. How did you talk to him about this?"

10. Decide how you will rate the candidates. We suggest a simple three-point system:
    - 0—the candidate does not have the required skill
    - 1—the candidate has the basic skill
    - 2—the candidate exceeds the required skill level
11. Assign a weight to the various skills based on their importance for the position. Interpersonal skills are more important for a customer service representative than software skills. The opposite might be true for an accountant. The easiest way to do this is to take 100 points and distribute the points among the different skills based on their importance. You can then multiply your rating by the weight for each skill and compute a numerical score for each candidate after the interview.
12. Plan each interview carefully. Give the candidates sufficient notice. Try to schedule the meeting at their convenience. Make sure that they know how to reach your location and where to park. Make sure that they are greeted in a courteous and professional manner. You have to impress them—you want the best people to want to work for you. Besides, you never know when one of the candidates might become a customer or might be a relative of a customer. Schedule enough time for the interview, to make notes afterwards, and to evaluate the candidate after the meeting ends.
13. A good procedure to follow would be:
    a. Welcome the candidate and introduce yourself and other interviewers.
    b. Make small talk (i.e., the weather, the city, some funny story in the news) and offer a beverage to put the person at ease.
    c. Explain the interview format and why you will take notes.
    d. Clarify the background data using closed-ended questions.
    e. Probe using the behavioral and situational interview questions.
    f. Take good notes even if you have to pause for a few seconds while you write.
    g. Invite the candidate to ask questions about the job and the organization.

    h. Tell the candidate when a decision will be made and when the candidate can expect to hear from you next. Stick with the time frame or call the candidate to explain when they will hear if there will be a delay. If a second interview or testing is required, schedule it after the first interview. Whenever possible, do all of the screening at one time.

    i. Thank the applicant for taking the time to interview.

14. Give the candidates time to think about their answers. When you ask more complicated open-ended questions about their past experiences, it takes longer to think about the answer and formulate the response.

15. If more than one person will make the decision as to which candidate to hire, it makes sense to have two to three people interview each candidate at one time. This is called panel interviewing and research has shown that this approach can improve the reliability of an interview. It must be the same group for each candidate. The responsibility for developing the questions can be shared after the skills have been identified and agreed upon. Following the interview, the interviewers should evaluate the candidate together.

16. When evaluating a candidate after the interview, you will use the information reported by the candidate and observations that you made during the interview. Do not use information that is not related to the job or make conclusions that you cannot substantiate. In your notes, provide specific useful information like, "She demonstrated a system of monitoring course scheduling." Do not write, "She showed know-how." Say, "He asked detailed questions about safety equipment and procedures in effect," not "Cautious." After three interviews, the candidates may begin to look alike.

    Do not write down notes that are irrelevant like, "He is single," or "She has kids," or "He is dark skinned." If you ever find yourself involved in a discrimination lawsuit, your interview notes will either be your best defense or incriminating evidence as they can be subpoenaed. Keep your notes and make sure the evaluative comments are legal, job related, professional, and **useful** to you.

17. Develop and use an interview form. The following is a sample interview form that you might want to tailor to your purposes.

Sample Interview Form

Performance skill 1: _____   Weight: _____

Question 1: _____

_____

Right answer: _____

_____

Interview notes: _____

_____

_____

Question 2: _____

_____

Right answer: _____

_____

Interview notes: _____

_____

_____

Question 3: _____

_____

Right answer: _____

_____

Interview notes: _____

_____

_____

Rating on Performance skill 1: _____ x _____ (weight) = _____ points

Performance skill 2: _____   Weight: _____

Question 1: _____

_____

Right answer: _____

_____

Interview notes: _____

_____

_____

Question 2: _____

Right answer: _____

Interview notes: _____

_____

Question 3: _____

Right answer: _____

Interview notes: _____

_____

_____

Rating on Performance skill 2: _____ x _____ **(weight) =** ____ **points**

Make additional copies for each performance skill being evaluated.

RESEARCH ON INTERVIEWING JOB CANDIDATES

Here are fifteen interviewing tips based on a review of published research on selection interviews.[2] These tips should enhance the reliability and validity of the interview process and improve reactions to interviews by job candidates.

1. Base interview questions on the job analysis (job description).
2. Ask each candidate the same questions.
3. Limit prompting, follow-up questioning, and elaboration on questions.
4. Use better questions (situational, behavioral, background, and job knowledge questions).
5. Use a longer interview or larger number of questions.
6. Control ancillary information (applications, resumes, transcripts, etc.). A well-designed vita, in terms of format, paper

quality, etc., can bias you even when the content (experience, publications, etc.) is no better than another candidate's.

 7. Do not allow questions from a candidate until after the interview.
 8. Rate each answer or use multiple scales.
 9. Use detailed anchored rating scales.
10. Take detailed notes.
11. Use multiple interviewers.
12. Use the same interviewer(s) across all candidates.
13. Do not discuss candidates or answers between interviews.
14. Provide extensive interviewing training.
15. Use statistical rather than clinical prediction.

HIRING THE BEST CANDIDATE

Put all of the information that you have gathered together. Keep in mind what technical and performance skills are most important. Remember that some technical skills can be taught. You can use a complex quantitative approach to determine the best candidate if that will work best for you. Gather together all of the information about the candidates and compare each on each tool used as part of your strategy. Which candidate received the highest scores on each tool? Which did best overall?

Chances are that if you did the recruiting and the initial screening well, you may have two candidates who look equally well qualified. You must now use your judgment to make the final decision. Here are some questions to ask yourself as you consider your choices:

- Which candidate complements the staff that you currently have?
- Does one candidate have a special skill or expertise or characteristic (for example, a second language) that would add value to the organization?
- Did one of the candidates offend you or others during the selection process?
- Did one of the candidates make you and others feel particularly comfortable during the interview?

- Are you sure that your comfort level with a candidate is not based on gender, race, ethnicity, religion, former college, neighborhood where the candidate grew up, etc.? If so, this comfort level is not a valid predictor of job performance. Put these biases aside and think about job-related criteria.
- Which candidate will make the best colleague over time?

NOTES

1. Uniform Guidelines on Employee Selection Procedures are published in the *Federal Register* 43, no. 166 (August 25, 1978): 38290–315.

2. M.A. Campion, D.K. Palmer, and J.E. Campion, "A Review of Structure in the Selection Interview," *Personnel Psychology* 50 (1997): 655–702.

SIX

Communicating Effectively

Communicating is the process by which information is exchanged and understood. Communicating effectively is as important to successful management and leadership as selecting the right employees for your work unit. Most of us would accept the notion that communication is vital; some of us might consider communication to be the essence of our professional lives, especially in view of the fact that managers typically spend up to 80 percent of their working days communicating with others. Unfortunately, however, relatively few of us would admit that we could benefit from an improvement in our communication skills. Surveys consistently reveal that nearly all of us consider ourselves to be better than average communicators, and that nearly 90 percent of managers rate their communication skills in the top 10 percent. Both of those are impossible, of course, but that is our perception because we are quick to blame others for instances of miscommunication. These facts signal trouble. Breakdowns in communication are consistently cited as one of the top reasons for leadership failures (not to mention one of the five most common causes of divorce).

The popular television show *The Office* depicts hilarious, yet painfully embarrassing, vignettes of a manager's bumbling attempts at communication with his employees. He considers himself to be an exemplary manager and frequently reflects with pride on his self-perceived ability to stay in touch with his subordinates. Yet, he is seemingly oblivious to the fact that he simply doesn't get it and is viewed by those same subordinates as clueless. Sit back and think—are you ever viewed that way by your subordinates or, worse, your supervisor? Simply put, most of us overestimate our communication ability, hardly pause to consider how we could improve it, and attribute communication breakdowns to our coworkers, colleagues, friends, relatives, and acquaintances. By so doing, we let poor communication become an Achilles' heel which limits our effectiveness as managers.

All of the sophisticated communication technology at our disposal does not guarantee effective communication, nor does it substitute for effective communication. What often happens instead of effective communication is information inundation, where an overload of communication magnifies inaccuracies, impedes proper interpretation, and fails to convey the necessary context. Sorry, managers—more isn't always better. What information technology does deliver is speed, but its evil twin is an increase in the timeliness of miscommunication as well.

COMMUNICATIONS CASE STUDY: TENERIFE

A tragic incident that happened three decades ago illustrates what can happen to even the most experienced professionals in the absence of effective communication, and we will refer to it at various places throughout this chapter. On March 27, 1977, a collision between two Boeing 747s on a foggy runway at Tenerife, Canary Islands, resulted in the loss of 583 lives. It still stands as the worst aviation accident in history; in terms of fatalities, it was the most deadly incident until the events of 9/11.

Although many factors contributed to the accident, the fact remains that the most probable cause of the accident was that one of the aircraft involved initiated a takeoff without having received clearance from the tower, according to the 1978 report by ALPA (Air Line Pilots Association). The ALPA report named the pilot of the KLM aircraft, Captain Jacob van Zanten, as the party most responsible for the accident. Captain van Zanten was KLM's chief training officer for Boeing 747s and was one of the company's most experienced pilots. He was also the public face of KLM, with cockpit photos of him in uniform at the controls appearing frequently in the company's advertising and promotion literature. A seasoned veteran of commercial flying, he started his career with KLM flying DC-3s in 1951 at the tender age of twenty-four. Experienced as he was, however, he missed several opportunities to communicate effectively, any single one of which would most likely have averted the entire disaster.

The events that put the disaster in motion started hours earlier. Because of a bomb threat that resulted in the closure of the primary airport at Grand Canary, a number of flights had been diverted to the much smaller Los Rodeos airport at the neighboring island of Tenerife. The taxiways and facilities there quickly became overcrowded. Delays inevitably caused stress and impatience. When aircraft were finally allowed to leave, Captain van Zanten's was the first in line, followed by the Pan Am jumbo jet. Congestion on the adjacent tarmac required departing aircraft to back-taxi, a procedure rarely used at commercial airports and one that necessitated aircraft to taxi down a single runway, turn completely around, and take off in the opposite direction. The control tower instructed the KLM aircraft to proceed down the runway, followed by the Pan Am aircraft, which would back-taxi until it could turn onto a clear portion of the taxiway to facilitate the KLM aircraft's takeoff. Around the same time, dense fog had descended on the airport, covering the runway and resulting in extremely poor visibility. Neither air crew could see the others' aircraft, nor could the control tower see either jumbo jet after they had proceeded down the runway. Further, the airport was not equipped with ground tracking radar to help controllers do their jobs.

At that point, Captain van Zanten's evident impatience escalated because of time pressures to take off within accepted air crew rest parameters. Once positioned at the end of the runway and turned around to face the oncoming Pan Am aircraft, the KLM crew then requested and received air traffic control route clearance—*not* takeoff clearance. However, because the route clearance was given so late in the procedural sequence that precedes a take-off, it was apparently mistaken by Captain van Zanten for takeoff clearance. The KLM copilot then radioed the control tower with the nonstandard and ambiguous phrase that "we are now at take off," meaning that the aircraft was starting to actually take off, and the control tower replied with "O.K., stand by for takeoff, I will call you," also nonstandard but clearly indicating that control tower personnel thought that meant that the flight was merely in position for takeoff and awaiting permission to do so.

Analysis of the KLM cockpit voice recorder recovered after the accident clearly revealed that Captain van Zanten thought he had been cleared for takeoff by the control tower. In fact, personnel in the control tower had not granted such clearance and were under the impression that the KLM aircraft was stationary at the end of the runway and awaiting proper clearance for takeoff. They did not know that the KLM flight had initiated its takeoff and was heading down the runway. The cockpit voice recorder also exposed the fact that the other members of the KLM air crew expressed hesitation to question Captain van Zanten's authority and decisions.

It was precisely at that moment that the Pan Am crew, during the final exchange between the KLM crew and the control tower, transmitted their awareness of a potentially dangerous situation and radioed "And we're still taxiing down the runway." Either of those two final transmissions—one from the control tower and one from the Pan Am air crew—should have alerted KLM to stop; however, apparently both the tower and Pan Am had made their transmissions almost simultaneously and thus neither was received intelligibly by KLM except for the tower's "O.K.," followed by the squeal of radio interference. The Pan Am crew hastily attempted to turn off the runway as quickly as possible when they sensed that a disaster was imminent. Moments later, the outbound KLM, attempting frantically to takeoff after finally sighting the other aircraft directly in its path, slammed broadside into the Pan Am. The KLM was engulfed by a fireball and all persons aboard were killed. Most of the passengers on the Pan Am were also killed, but some, including the air crew, escaped their burning aircraft.

How could such an experienced pilot have been responsible for colliding broadside with a taxiing Pan Am 747 without having receiving clearance for takeoff? As the summary above indicates, there were certainly factors other than a lack of effective communication that contributed to this disaster. Let us examine this incident step by step and list the reasons why it occurred:

1. An unexpected emergency situation had occurred—people were thrown off their routines and had to adapt to less than ideal circumstances.
2. Crowding caused tension.
3. Delays caused schedules to slip, which carried consequences.
4. People's tempers flared.
5. Time pressures caused pilots to exercise less caution than they should have.
6. An unusual procedure to clear the Tenerife airfield was used.
7. Nonstandard phraseology was used.
8. Visibility on the ground was almost zero.
9. A pilot had mistakenly thought he had been given permission to depart—he heard what he wanted to hear, not what he should have heard.
10. Radio interference squelched a critical transmission.
11. A pilot's expertise caused him to be overconfident about the situation and his abilities, and to trust his own judgment without verification and rechecking.
12. Other flight crew members deferred to the pilot's judgment because they did not wish to question his authority.
13. The use of feedback was virtually nonexistent.

However, this case also demonstrates clearly and compellingly how the occurrence of a single effective instance of communication would have averted the disaster. Framed in reverse, these events illustrate the importance of effective communication by depicting the tragic consequences that can happen in its absence.

Most of us do not operate daily in such life-and-death situations, but we certainly function in an environment of unanticipated events and time pressures which provide a parallel to the Tenerife disaster. Organizations are complex and opportunities for miscommunication abound. As managers, we can become more effective communicators by adhering to a few simple principles.

1. **Recognize the Barriers.** First, understand the delicate nature of the communication process—and the noise and barriers that exist.

   The communication process is far from straightforward, with numerous sources of potential error. As we saw in the Tenerife example, the communication process is susceptible to interference. For even a simple, two-way exchange, the initiator of a message (the sender) must mentally develop the message to be sent, encode it into some common language that will be understood by the recipient (the receiver), and transmit it by some means (voice, picture, physical, or electronic). At that point, the message must take some pathway to the receiver, actually be received, then be decoded to be understood. The receiver must then develop a response, encode it, and transmit it back to the initiating party. Throughout this process, noise exists that can hamper the communication process. Noise means anything that can cause an impediment to the transmission, receipt, or understanding of a message—be it physical, cognitive, or whatever. It cannot be overemphasized that this process is not nearly as robust as managers assume.

   Take the simple example of a manager telling a subordinate who has just arrived "thanks for being on time." What does that mean, exactly? Well, it could mean exactly that—an expression of appreciation on the part of a manager to a subordinate. On the other hand, to the subordinate, it might come across as a backhanded way of chastisement for not being on time, particularly in the context of other preceding events (such as being tardy the week before). If the manager tends to be sarcastic, that might in fact be what it means. If the message is sent in a noisy environment, say, a shop floor, it might be received as "next time be on time," or, alternatively, "you're on time," or even "right on time." What is the receiver to make of such a message? Is she or he being reprimanded (in the first case), praised (in the third case), or subject to ambiguity (in the second case)? This type of ambiguity happens all of the time, so it is hardly surprising that social psychologists who study communication effectiveness estimate that there is usually around a 50 percent loss of meaning in the transmission of messages in organizational settings. In the Tenerife disaster, what did "we are now at take off" signify to the control tower? Certainly something quite different from what it was intended to communicate.

Communication gains complexity rapidly as organizations grow, straining an already fragile process by being exposed to more opportunities for ambiguity or breakdown. Two people communicate with a single channel ($1 \rightarrow 2$); three people have three possible channels ($1 \rightarrow 2$, $2 \rightarrow 3$, and $3 \rightarrow 1$); four people have six possible channels ($1 \rightarrow 2$, $2 \rightarrow 3$, $3 \rightarrow 4$, $1 \rightarrow 3$, $2 \rightarrow 4$, and $1 \rightarrow 4$); and so on. As the size of an organization increases arithmetically, the number of possible communication channels increases exponentially. The sheer number of communication conduits can result in garbled messages, similar to what happens in the game where children sit in a circle, whisper a message in the ear of their neighbor, and what results after it has gone around the circle is completely different in meaning that what started. In the interest of time we often accept the erroneous message instead of confirming it, assuming that we know its true meaning. Garbled messages are often worse than messages that aren't received at all, as the Tenerife disaster illustrates.

Barriers to effective communication exist within and around us. Effective communicators know that they need to recognize them and deal with them. Some of those barriers are individual and some are organizational. Individual barriers involve interpersonal dynamics. They include things such as language differences—and that means the "language" specific to our own disciplines as well. Semantics pose another barrier; the meaning of words, abbreviations, and acronyms might differ between people, causing confusion or mistakes in interpretation. Selective perception is another individual barrier to communication; we attend to what we are attuned to pay attention to, and ignore the rest.

Intellectual rigidity that results from people having their minds already made up about something, resulting in their inability or unwillingness to consider any other information, is another barrier, as are inconsistent nonverbal cues, which we will discuss at length later in this chapter. Organizational barriers to effective communication include status and power differences; lower-power individuals are often reluctant to communicate bad news to higher-power individuals, who in turn might not be inclined to pay much attention to them anyway. Differing and sometimes conflicting departmental goals also pose barriers to communication because they tend to limit our understanding of others' problems and needs. Another organizational barrier exists when communication channels are insufficient or unsuited to allow proper coordination of tasks that must be accomplished. Those channels often filter the information that people transmit and receive, thereby reducing its meaning considerably. A final organizational barrier can result from people simply using the wrong channel to communicate information.

We discuss trade-offs in communication channel choice below, but we are often constrained in our choice by established communication channels that have been selected for us. Those formal communication channels tend to follow traditional lines of hierarchy and reporting relationships, and tend to emphasize vertical information flows. Organizations in recent years have focused on creating formal lateral communication channels, which operate more quickly and, in most cases, reliably.

2. **Select the Proper Communication Channel.** The channels that we choose for our communicating must be chosen with care. When given the choice, most managers implicitly favor channels that are efficient over those that might be more effective. That's a natural default, actually, because we are constantly pressured to increase efficiency as a means to a healthier

financial bottom line. Communication differs greatly from finance, however, and the irony here is that most (but not all) communication channels are relatively inexpensive. Let's examine communication channels and their respective attributes.

The most efficient communication channels are those that are impersonal and static, such as bulletins, form letters, and general memos. They are very inexpensive to distribute, and they can elicit a lot of attention with a few words. They are most appropriate for communicating clear, routine, simple information to a large number of people through an organization. The downside is that although they can reach far and deep, they lack richness. Scheduling a company picnic? Richness isn't an issue, so impersonal static communication channels fit the bill.

Personal static communication channels are slightly less efficient, but provide a degree of richness. They include such things as individualized letters, e-mail, text messaging, and personal memos. They are most appropriate for communicating personalized messages such as requests for information, directives, and clarification. Like impersonal static communication channels, they are unidirectional.

Interactive communication channels represent a major increase in the richness of information exchange. Examples of such channels include the telephone and instant messaging. They are not as efficient because they are limited in their reach and they require managerial attention throughout their use, but when reciprocity is required they are far more effective than a series of static messages. Need to enter into a dialogue or real-time exchange of information? Interactive communication channels are most appropriate.

Finally, when richness is an absolute necessity, the appropriate communication channel is a meeting. Meetings are criticized for their inefficiency, and in fact most meetings are. However, when the information to be exchanged is nonroutine, unique, or requires lots of explanation, meetings should not be avoided merely for the sake of efficiency. Many messages are difficult to deliver or receive, or perhaps ambiguous in nature, and require that managers see how they affect their recipients so that they can respond appropriately to nonverbal cues. In such cases, meetings are the appropriate communication channel. Managers today can make meetings more efficient through the use of information technology (e.g., teleconferencing), so inefficiency is becoming less of an issue than it has been in the recent past.

Captain van Zanten allowed efficiency to trump richness. He was in a hurry and heard what he wanted to during his exchange with the control tower. In fact, he essentially controlled the conversation rather than engaging in an interactive dialog. Given the ground conditions at Tenerife, he would have been better served to make certain that he participated more evenly in a careful, effective exchange of information that was explicitly nonroutine. Further, he did not follow up when he heard the squelched radio messages that occurred when the control tower and the Pan Am aircraft attempted to communicate simultaneously on the single communication channel shared by all, thereby generating interference that masked any intelligible messages. People "step on" each other in a similar manner constantly in their daily conversations; we have all experienced that when trying to talk simultaneously with somebody on the other end of our telephone line. It doesn't work very well. Captain van Zanten needed to take a step back and make certain he understood precisely what was happening on his runway.

3. **Listen More Than You Talk.** Active listening is the key to successful communication. Time and again, research and experience reveals that the most important aspect of effective communication is also our least developed communication skill—the ability to listen. Or, as a wise person once said, "communication is not about *oral* ability; it is about *aural* ability." Simply put, the best communicators are those who listen more than they speak. After all, communication involves the *reciprocal* exchange of information. We need to ensure that our messages are being received, but to do so we must listen to

others' responses. The fundamental problem is that we humans love to talk but hate to listen. If that doesn't describe you, then you are indeed the rare manager because it has been said that the human ear is our least developed "muscle." Even if we master the monologue, we seldom become equally adept at dialog. To become a good listener requires work and dedication because it isn't natural for most managers to assume a passive role in information exchange. Here is the news—listening should not be a passive activity. Good listeners are anything but passive. Active listening is the ticket.

Active listeners support those who are speaking or otherwise transmitting information and make them better at that activity. For example, active listeners understand the value of eye contact, so they fix their attention on the sender to let the sender know that they are interested in the message so much that it is the only thing that matters to them. They exhibit appropriate gestures and other nonverbal cues to support the conversation, encouraging the sender to continue or, alternatively, suggesting to them that they need to explain their message differently. Active listeners avoid making gestures that distract the sender or suggest boredom. There's nothing quite so distracting as the habit of a boss whose gaze drifts off and whose hands stroke his tie, collar, hair, or ears in the middle of a conversation. The message being sent is that he has more pressing things on his mind. Active listeners take great pains not to interrupt the sender (a major no-no in effective communication), but they do take advantage of natural pauses and transition points to ask questions for clarification and to paraphrase the message back to the sender to confirm whether that was what he or she intended to say. At Tenerife, Captain van Zanten failed to be a good listener because he was in a hurry and not at all interested in hearing anything that would delay his departure from the airport.

It goes without saying that it is more than the appearance of interest that is important; active listeners concentrate hard on the sender and resist making premature judgments based on the information being provided. It is only human to start making interpretations as we assimilate information, so perhaps the most difficult skill to master in active listening is maintaining an open mind. If we don't work on that, we will filter information, thereby subconsciously restricting our consideration of its meaning. Good active listeners also work diligently to judge the content of a message, not its delivery. This is not as easy as it might seem, because we are always communicating in an environment where context directs or distracts our attention. To be a good active listener requires that we focus our attention on content rather than the delivery or the messenger.

Carl Rogers developed the active listening technique use by psychologists in clinical settings. One aspect of this technique involves repeating a speaker's words back in order to clarify information. Managers can use that technique as well. For example, a manager/listener might say, "It sounds like you had prepared the report on time." The employee/speaker might respond, "Yes, I did, but then I found more information." The manager might then say, "It sounds like you felt frustrated by the time constraints and the need to produce an accurate and complete summary," to which the employee might then respond, "Absolutely, it is important to me that I do my job thoroughly, and I would have appreciated a little more time in this case." This exchange provided the manager with additional information because she allowed the employee to clarify how he felt in this situation and why he did what he did.

Too often, managers will try to make subordinates feel better by saying "You don't have to worry about it," which does nothing to help the subordinate. Managers must acknowledge the feelings of their employees, allow them to have those feelings, and then provide honest, direct feedback that they can use to perform more effectively in the future.

4. **ABC—Always Be Clear.** Simple, unambiguous language is always best if you wish to enhance the effectiveness of communication. However, most of us fall into the trap of either elevating our language to sound erudite, or using shorthand to more quickly dispense with a message. Both of those situations

impede effective communication. In the case of the former, using "big words" when others would suffice guarantees that a significant percentage of those to whom you are attempting to communicate will not understand you. For example, if you say "using this option will obviate the currently installed data base," how will most people interpret it? Obviate means to prevent, preclude, or avert, but many people will think that it means to make obvious or to complement, especially considering the context in which it is used. Moreover, if your audience is uncertain about the meaning of your words, what are the odds that they will stop you and ask? People don't want to look uneducated, so you can't rely on very many of them asking what "obviate" means.

Experts tell us that we should write (and speak) to *express*, not to *impress*. That is good advice. When in doubt, use simple language. Don't assume that use of vernacular, acronyms, or jargon will make for effective communication, either. Unless you are positive that the people with whom you are communicating will understand their meaning, back off and use simple, straightforward English and standard phraseology. Again, the goal of effective communication is not to make you appear savvy to the latest terminology, it is to direct, guide, or influence others to achieve the desired result. The KLM copilot's use of the nonstandard phrase "...we are now at take off" introduced ambiguity into a situation that could tolerate precious little of it, thereby precipitating the tragic events that followed.[1]

Simplicity should reign supreme; save complex messages for those occasions where technical or situational necessities dictate. In addition to clarity, brevity is a feature that accompanies effective communication. Many of us substitute quantity for quality, which invariably erodes the effectiveness of our communication. Developing a treatise on whether an employee should take a particular action is far less effective than simply telling that employee "yes" or "no," with additional explanation coming later, if needed, as a learning device.

5. **Consider Nonverbal Communication.** If you want to tap into most managers' source of pride, ask them about their ability to

interpret nonverbal communication—a.k.a. "body language." Because we often read body language correctly, we soon develop a belief that we are experts in the field. How wrong that assumption would be. Nonverbal communication is transmitted through actions, behavior, and gestures, and not spoken or written words. As such, nonverbal communication never appears in static communications such as e-mails and memos. It can arise from time to time in telephone conversations; for example, pregnant pauses, sighs, elevated volume, and change in intonation are all nonverbals. Nonverbal communication primarily enters organizational communication during direct, personal communication in the presence of others.

Studies suggest that over 90 percent of the meaning we derive from communication comes from nonverbal cues presented by the other party. Nonverbal communication often reveals our true thoughts and feelings whereas verbal communication can be more easily masked to conceal them. As such, nonverbal cues provide managers with a potential source of richness for effective communication; nonverbal cues can supplement verbal messages, thereby validating them, or they can contradict verbal messages, sending mixed signals that force us to choose between different parts of a message—and we generally choose the nonverbal portions. Such choices can lead us to erroneous conclusions, which is unfortunate but curable if we use those mixed signals as an opportunity to probe for additional meaning or clarification. Sometimes nonverbal cues can be misinterpreted.

For example, when somebody crosses their arms over their chest when receiving a message, the usual interpretation is that they resist it or don't believe it. When people look around when others are speaking to them, it is generally assumed that they are expressing boredom or lack of interest. Both of those interpretations might be wrong. People cross their arms for other reasons—perhaps the room is chilly or they are nervous and simply don't know what to do with their arms. A coworker once sat back in his chair and stared at the ceiling while listening, closing his eyes tightly and giving the impression that he wished he was in another place. Actually, it was his way of concentrating on the message and thinking about his response. The point is, don't assume that the nonverbal cues given by others fit the accepted pattern, especially if you don't know them very well.

6. **Don't Disregard Informal Communication Channels.** In the movie *Jurassic Park,* one of the taglines is, "Life will find a way." So it is with informal communication channels, or those that exist outside of and separate from the formal communication channels established by our organizations. They will pop up all around us, and any efforts we take to stamp them out as if they are small brush fires will be fruitless. Some informal channels are established by friends and colleagues who share something in common—often their relative position in the hierarchy, education, life experiences, and common interests or circumstances.

Additionally, some informal groups serve to protect their members by providing information. For example, long-term employees tend to form informal networks which look out for their mutual interests. Other common informal groups include employees who start on the same day, African-American employees, janitors, and administrative assistants. Administrative assistants frequently know important information before executives do because they usually handle the communications. Executives will often speak very openly in front of janitors without giving much thought to what they are saying— perhaps assuming that janitors will not understand. Another group, retirees, can be very knowledgeable since current employees, including executives, feel that they can be trusted with confidential information.

Such channels tend to be an extremely rapid and efficient means of information transfer, and they can often augment formal communication channels. Why, then, do managers spend so much time trying to eliminate or neutralize them? One reason is that although they are fast, that speed can result in the spread of misinformation (read: gossip chains) and other information of questionable reliability. Another reason is that they threaten managers' status and power. Both of those reasons are shortsighted, however, and managers can take advantage of the coexistence of informal communication channels if they use a little initiative.

One of the techniques managers can do to exploit informal communication channels is to deliberately overcommunicate, sending a consistent message through formal channels with sufficient repetition so that it is swiftly transferred and retransmitted through informal channels. This works especially well when the informal channel is a grapevine. Consistency and repetition are essential because by flooding the organization channels with messages that drive home the same point, incorrect messages, rumors, and other miscommunications are overwhelmed or swept aside. Another technique managers can use to tap into the informal communication network is "management by wandering around." Although certainly nothing new, that practice allows managers to exchange information with individuals or groups of subordinates who might not otherwise be represented in formal channels. Finally, an open-door policy that invites employees in to speak with managers is an effective means of communication because it strips away intermediaries who might filter messages or impart so much "spin" to them as to render them useless.

7. **Make Feedback Work.** One of the most important facets of effective communication is the use of feedback, which has been shown repeatedly to be underutilized by managers. Managers who develop their skills in giving *and receiving* feedback can improve their effectiveness as well as establish a climate of mutual respect with their subordinates. Managers are hesitant to give feedback because of the negative consequences that it connotes; namely, fear of causing embarrassment or a "scene," discomfort, anxiety about how the recipient will respond, and possible inability to handle such a response in a professional manner. Feedback, however, doesn't always have to be negative. Instead, it can be reinforcing. People appreciate positive feedback and it has been shown to be an effective source of motivation. If managers use positive feedback, people will be

far less resentful on those occasions when they must give negative feedback.

To be effective, feedback must be constructive. First and foremost, it must be timely. Giving late feedback is probably worse than giving no feedback at all because it might be interpreted as a petty way for somebody to criticize another person when she/he has nothing better to do. It might also have no impact if given late because the cause-and-effect relationship has been lost in time and possibly overridden by more pressing problems dictated by the current situation. Feedback should *always* be kept on a professional level, *never* on a personal level. If it becomes personal, it loses its effectiveness (best case), puts the recipient on the defensive, and invites resistance or hostility (worst case). On a related note, feedback should address specific behaviors and actions that can be controlled or otherwise acted upon, not general feelings or attitudes that are far less tangible and probably beyond the capability of the recipient to change—even if she or he wished to. Feedback should be goal oriented, with a clear path and objectives delineated to the recipient to enable them to get back on track.

Feedback should be a two-way street. Managers can ensure that feedback is understood by making it reciprocal, not unidirectional. After all, if you give it, you should be prepared to receive it with grace, dignity, and maturity. Allowing subordinates to give you feedback will go a long way toward establishing trust and a healthy working relationship, provided they follow the same rules and keep their feedback constructive. Make every attempt to not get defensive. Don't interrupt or overreact, and ask for clarification so that you understand fully what is being expressed to you. Open-ended questions are most appropriate to expand the discussion as necessary, and close-ended questions are most appropriate when probing for specifics. To conclude feedback sessions, summarize the key points, actions to be taken, and a timeline for the next session. Make feedback part of your effective communication skill set.

Feedback is built into aviation communication, and in the Tenerife disaster it is obvious that it was not used properly.

Had established communication procedures been followed at any one of several junctures in the sequence of events leading up to the tragedy, it would likely have been avoided.

YOU CAN DO IT

We have offered several suggestions to help managers improve their communication effectiveness. Each of the principles described in this chapter is under our control. Implicit in almost any discussion of communicating in organizations is a basic trade-off: effectiveness vs. efficiency. When facing such a trade-off decision, too many managers default to efficiency, assuming that abbreviated messages will be understood or, if not, they will be queried for additional information. That decision, usually made without much thought, underscores a tremendous problem. As we have learned from the tragic events that took place at an otherwise unremarkable airport at Tenerife, that is an erroneous assumption. Communicating requires resources, most significantly managerial time and attention. Well, isn't that our job in the first place? Instead of considering communication as a trade-off, we would be better served viewing it as a series of choices. Sure, we want to be concise and thorough. We need to make certain that the other party understands our message, and give them an opportunity to acknowledge that understanding. We need to ensure that we get it right.

NOTES

1. As often accompanies a preventable disaster, some good came from it in the form of changes that were made to communication procedures. Among those changes was a worldwide requirement that all commercial flight crews and control towers use standard phrases in English.

SEVEN

Understanding and Motivating Employees

Humans have been trying to understand and motivate other humans for thousands of years. After all of this time, the only thing that we know for sure is that we are all different, different things motivate different people, you can please some of the people—well, you know. That being said, there are things which can be done which will help you manage better and we are going to share many concrete suggestions. You have to decide if these tips fit your personal communication and work styles, will work in your specific environment, whether you personally can pull them off, and if you care to try. We will break this into three parts: Understanding others, motivating employees, and providing performance feedback.

UNDERSTANDING OTHERS

Listen to and observe employees. What are you looking and listening for?

1. Does the employee interact frequently with coworkers and you? *You can get clues about whether the employee is an extrovert who works best with others or an introvert who will work best alone.*

2. What does the employee talk about? Is it strictly work or does he discuss his family and friends? *This will provide more clues about introversion and extroversion. You want to find how to set up the work environment and which assignments will work best for this individual. What does he value?*

3. Does the employee show pride in her job, her profession, coworkers, and the company? *Clues will come from how she describes her job to others, and talks to and about customers. Bad feelings about a job typically come from poor relationships with bosses and coworkers or pay dissatisfaction. Even difficult and unpleasant work environments are respected by employees if they are managed well and paid fairly. This type of information will help you determine whether the job is right for the individual and whether you are doing a good job managing her. Negative attitudes about a job, profession, or company often reflect the feelings of others, including the manager. In other words, perhaps you need an attitude adjustment if an employee's negative comments about a client reflect your feelings.*

4. Does he easily and comfortably approach you and other managers? Does he say and do things which make it appear that he feels he is part of a team? For example, does he share opinions regarding the way the work could be improved? Or does he act like he feels disrespected? For example, does he comment on his lack of power and control over his work to you or to coworkers? *Workers who feel subordinate to management may not be team players, which is critical to identifying problems and making improvements. You may need to increase your contact with him, asking him about his work and treating him as the expert on what he does.*

5. When she talks about having fun, who and what does she talk about? Does she enjoy being with others, NASCAR, partying, eating, traveling, reading, or skiing? Does she like sports—golf, tennis, volleyball? Or the arts—plays, concerts, museum visits—or the outdoors—hiking, beach weekends, kayaking? Or, does she enjoy being with her family—reunions, trips with her children, weekends with her husband? *This will give you a link to build cohesiveness with you and others in the department.*

A new employee can be directed to the others who love to travel. It will give you a wealth of material to use to talk about when you see her in the cafeteria or at the mall after work. Even introverted bosses must make an effort to build friendly relationships with their direct reports. Finding common ground makes it much easier.

6. Who are his best friends at work? Or, does he stay to himself? With whom does he have lunch, take breaks, or see after work? To whom does he go with problems? Who is mentoring him? *Creating effective work teams is often difficult. However, knowing which employees get along and work well together is one indicator of how well they will interact on a work team. After recruiting members of a project team years ago, one of the authors was asked how she chose the team. They expected her to talk about their professional specialties, how they represented various levels in the organization, because they had good contacts, etc. Instead, she told them the truth. She picked people she liked and respected. A group made up of people who like and respect each other can accomplish any task or solve any problem. Productive employees are usually attracted to other productive employees. On those rare occasions that a coworker is liked, but is not respected professionally, he probably won't do any harm to the project. Note that this advice is based on the assumption that goof-offs are not picked as project managers.*

7. What kind of music does she listen to as she works? What radio station is playing in the area? What is her favorite TV program or movie? What Web sites does she visit? Is her desktop a picture of a movie star, or a child, or a news Web site? What type of calendar does she display at her desk? *Every hint of her interests provides a springboard to beginning a conversation which may evolve into a discussion of a work project or a way to integrate her personal interests into her work.*

8. Does he talk about his college, his current coursework or training programs, or a professional book he is reading? Does he talk about what he is learning or the college's new facilities or the football team? *Managers need to know who is soaking up knowledge and needs more training or formal education. Maybe you should be encouraging him to pursue an MBA, go to the technical school for additional training, or read a book on a specific topic.*

Observing and listening to employees at work will give you the best insights into what makes people tick. There are other methods which have their advantages and disadvantages.

For example, many organizations use attitude surveys. These can be useful in some situations; however, we have found some common problems with them. First, not one single employee on the planet believes that their answers are really anonymous. You can assure them, not require names, eliminate all identifying information, etc., but they will believe that you can find out who said what. As a result, employees are not honest on attitude surveys. Are they paranoid? Not really. We used an attitude survey several years ago which contained no identifying information, whatsoever. In a meeting summarizing the results, we brought the original surveys in order to share some of the written comments. One of the managers saw the survey on the top of the stack and began speculating about who had a pen like that. Here is what the rest of the books won't tell you, but everyone knows. Managers will take negative comments, ratings, and suggestions from attitude surveys and try to figure out which employee said what, even when they cannot see the ink. Against all reason, that speculation affects their behavior toward employees. Your employees know this, and because of it many do not give honest responses on attitude surveys.

Many trainers use personality assessments to help managers and work teams better understand each other. We have found the Myers-Briggs Personality Inventory to be particularly useful. However, only trainers who have completed the certification for the instrument can effectively help you understand the results and what to do with them. There are many other tools available to trainers and managers. Most are simply fluff and do not provide useful information about personality at work. On occasion, managers will ask psychologists to administer more accurate personality assessments like MMPI (Minnesota Multiphasic Personality Inventory), which reveals much more than an average business manager should know about his employees. Target Stores ran into a problem a few years ago because they used the MMPI for selection, but the people who were hired did not want that kind of information left in their employee files. The bottom line is that a few personality tools are appropriate for team building and increasing understanding of others, but managers must be very careful about interpreting and using the results.

At the risk of making understanding others look easier than it is for some, it can be done. Watch, listen, pay attention, and think about people. We give clues about ourselves every minute, which observant managers can use to make better decisions. However, don't rely too heavily on your early interactions, because we all act differently around other people until we get used to them and begin to feel safe. When we feel safe, our true behavior and personalities emerge.

MOTIVATING EMPLOYEES

There is a school of thought that suggests that managers cannot motivate their employees. Although we do not completely agree with this philosophy, we do advocate hiring employees who are interested in the work they will do and want to work for the company. That might seem obvious, but it is not. Many of us want to work in a particular geographic area and we may even take jobs we do not want in undesirable organizations in order to live near our family or our spouse's family or where the skiing is good or where the weather is nice year round. So, during the hiring process do everything you can to ensure that the new hire likes the work first and foremost.

Having given that disclaimer, what can managers do to influence the motivation of others? We are going to provide many specific ideas for you to try. When we talk about motivation, we are essentially looking for employees who do what we want them to do, work hard, and persist at that work. Managers commonly say that some of their employees are "not motivated." Nothing could be further from the truth. We are all motivated by some interest or activity. What managers want is for the employees to be motivated to do what they want them to do. It is accurate to say that some of anyone's employees are "not motivated to do the work that must be done."

An important concept that has emerged recently in the management literature is self-efficacy. Self-efficacy refers to the belief that a worker has that he is capable of successfully completing a task. Research suggests that when we believe that we are capable, we perform at a higher level. Self-efficacy comes from several sources:

1. Our past successful experiences.
2. Our observations of other people and our assessment of how they succeeded or failed and how that compares with ourselves. In other words, if a colleague wrote an excellent report, we may feel more efficacious because we work as hard as that individual.
3. Encouragement from our managers and coworkers.
4. Physiological arousal. In other words, we may actually feel excited about a particular task ahead of us because of our feelings toward our team. A good example of that would be military units where soldiers do superhuman feats because they feel responsible for their "band of brothers" and sisters.

Managers can play a role in developing self-efficacy by understanding how it develops. For example, we can break assignments into small pieces, allowing our subordinates to have incremental successes. Managers can remind employees of past successes. Managers can suggest that employees observe successful workers in their units and learn from their efforts. They can also talk about how others overcome limitations to succeed. Of course, providing encouragement and letting workers know that the management team believes in their ability to succeed is critical. Pep talks may seem corny to some of us, but they work. Getting people excited and feeling that they are part of something bigger than themselves can be a very effective strategy for building self-efficacy.

One of the best approaches to motivation is goal setting. Review Chapter 3 for detailed information about the goal-setting process. Here is some more information about motivation.

A common myth is that people who are close to their families cannot be motivated by work. This is an accusation often used as an excuse not to hire or promote women. Current research has found that younger men and women are more interested in a balanced work life (i.e., the desire to spend more time with their families and personal interests in proportion with their careers) than previous generations. This trend has been used as evidence that younger workers are not as motivated or lack a work ethic. We do not buy these accusations. Employees who are motivated by caring, interest, and time with their families typically work very hard because they want to take good care of their spouses and children in order to maintain their jobs. However, they are not open to meaningless face time in their workplace. We may actually see greater efficiency as younger workers find ways to finish their work and still maintain healthy lifestyles. With any luck, the old-style workaholic who puts in sixty hours and dies at fifty of a heart attack will be gone.

Equity theory comes from an old philosophical idea which has applications to everyday management. Basically, equity theory suggests that humans are constantly comparing their work input (e.g., the job that they do, the amount of training and education they have, how long they work) with their work outputs (e.g., pay, benefits, perks, satisfaction). When we feel that there is an imbalance, we will correct it. For example, if we believe that we are giving more than we are getting, we will cut back on the amount and the quality of the work that we do or we will look for another job. The research suggests that this is true. In fact, the research into animal behavior has found that most animals have this same instinct. Somehow, the mind keeps track. We do this in both our personal and professional lives.

In addition to comparing our own inputs and outputs, we also track those of others who are like us in terms of job, age, experience, etc. If we see that someone else is working harder and getting more pay, we will increase our effort in order to earn more. If we see that another is getting more with less effort, we may cut back on the time and effort that we expend on our jobs. In addition, we now know that good employees who are dissatisfied due to equity issues are more likely to find another job than they are to cut back on the quality of the work that they do.

This raises another important issue which managers must understand. It appears that our basic personality determines our work ethic. Research has shown that conscientious people perform better across jobs than people who are not conscientious. Often, managers talk about conscientiousness as an attitude—accusing workers of "not being conscientious"—as if they are doing it on purpose. Actually, conscientiousness is a personality trait. Personality traits are in part innate and in part learned at a very early age.

The idea that conscientiousness and all of the other personality dimensions that drive work behavior are personality traits is an important concept. Because it means that managers cannot fundamentally change workers. Workers cannot change their own personalities, either. They aren't being bad, mean, stubborn, careless, unmotivated, lazy, etc. In this case, they simply are not conscientious. Period! What can a manager do? Here are a few suggestions.

1. Recruit and hire conscientious employees. When you are hiring employees, use personality testing to identify conscientious candidates. Hire them.
2. Use personality testing to identify the strengths and weaknesses of current employees. Hire a psychologist to explain how their personality type affects interactions at work.
3. Use more supervision and guidance when working with employees who lack conscientiousness. This means that you must monitor their work more closely and provide more feedback as they perform.
4. You may need to do additional training for these types of employees.
5. You may need to tell them more than once what needs to be done and how to do it.
6. Identify the strengths of each worker's personality and use them to perform tasks where those strengths can be utilized. For example, if someone is introverted, that person will be better at tasks that require working alone and having decision making authority.

Work Design

About forty years ago, a new trend in management emerged based on specific characteristics of particular jobs. This line of thinking challenged traditional methods of management, which mandated that jobs must be simple enough for trained chimps to perform because humans were lazy and simple minded and apt to commit errors, not to mention fraud. Essentially, what developed from this new thinking that maybe humans were not all idiots (we say only half jokingly) were concepts like job enrichment and job enlargement. These techniques make specific jobs bigger in the sense that each employee will have more than just one repetitive task and will have some responsibility. Of course, research followed. We found that workers were more satisfied when their jobs were enriched (i.e., made more interesting and fulfilling). And when workers are more satisfied, they are less likely to be absent, change jobs, and have accidents at work. When workers are more satisfied, we have an easier time hiring new workers. All of those outcomes are worth money in terms of cost and time savings.

In particular, two of the most important characteristics of enriched jobs are autonomy and feedback. Autonomy means that a worker has some decision making authority. If something goes wrong, the worker may decide how to handle it instead of having to go to a supervisor for permission or advice about what to do. When employees have autonomy, they tend to take more responsibility for the outcomes of their work. In other words, when employees are allowed to make choices, they tend to make those choices work or change their choices to practices which will work better. The level of autonomy should be based on the skill level of the employee. A new hire will probably have little. A worker with a year of experience may be asked to develop a solution, but run it by the boss before implementation. An experienced worker should decide, implement a solution, and report to the boss if the problem persists.

Feedback comes into play when a manager keeps a worker updated as to how she is performing. If she is performing well, she knows to continue behaving in the same way. If she is not performing well, she knows that she needs to change. If the feedback is detailed, honest and timely, she can make appropriate changes quickly and get herself back on track. Humans like that. It is necessary for survival. How much feedback is necessary, again, depends on the worker and the environment. If reports are automatically generated and distributed, that will serve as feedback. If the employee has made one minor error during a busy work day, she may not need to be told about it. If a new employee is making many mistakes, something is wrong and extensive feedback and more training is required.

In general, think about each of the jobs reporting to you—not the people, but the jobs. Would you like to do that job all day? If not, what could be done to make it more interesting and rewarding to the employee who holds the job? Ask them before you change it. They may love a tedious task now and then because they get a break—they do not have to think about work for a few minutes every day. There is nothing wrong with that. On the other hand, a day full of boring tasks is not a motivating job.

Rewards

In the United States, the annual merit increase (raise) is the most commonly used reward. The merit increase has averaged around 3.5–4.0 percent for about fifteen years. This is due, in large part, to low cost of living increases for the past two decades. Although we are all happy about the cost of living remaining stable, 3.5 percent raise pools do not give managers much leverage to use the merit increase as a motivational tool. We remember 16 percent raises which bought little, given inflation rates at the time, but felt like a generous recognition of performance. The bottom line is that money is not the best or most effective reward, but it is necessary. In other words, the annual raise is unlikely to get workers out of bed early, but if you do not give one, they will stay in bed later. This is just one of the many "Catch 22's" of managing. There are some basic rules of effective rewards and they are explained below.

1. The reward must be **available** to the manager to give. If you want to give an excellent worker a 15 percent raise, you probably cannot do it due to corporate guidelines. However, if you want to give a worker more freedom on his job, you can more easily do that, usually without corporate-level approval.
2. An effective reward is **visible.** When other workers can see the reward given to a colleague and when they know the reason it

was given, it has a motivational impact on many employees. Since merit increases are typically confidential, only the employee knows, and the reward therefore has less value to the organization as a means to motivate others. When performance bonuses are distributed based on sales levels which have been monitored and posted on a special web page for a month, everyone knows who got the bonus and why it was given. The impact is magnified.

3. In order for a reward to be effective, it must be **contingent upon performance.** When every employee gets a turkey at Thanksgiving, no one feels special about it. Of course, if you do not distribute the turkeys next year, everyone is mad. However, when the top customer representative who received no customer complaints the previous year wins a trip to the sales meeting in Miami, everyone thinks about how she did it and how great it would be for them to win the trip next year.

4. Effective rewards are **timely.** Unfortunately, merit increases are given once per year. If outstanding performance happens to coincide with the annual increase, it might be timely. Usually, however, it is not. In fact, a merit increase is just as likely to follow a mistake as it is likely to follow especially good performance. On the other hand, giving a worker more freedom on the job can be done as soon as he shows that he has earned it. That is timeliness. Use rewards that can be given when they are earned—praise, recognition, freedom, feedback, public acknowledgement of a job well done, etc.

5. It is important that rewards be **reversible.** There is some confusion about what that means. It means that the manager can stop giving it. Examples of reversible rewards are bonuses tied to specific instances of superior performance, praise and recognition, and sales commissions. Rewards that are not reversible are raises—the gift that keeps giving. Although technically possible and legal, few managers take salary increases back if the performance decreases. Usually the individual keeps the raise forever. In fact, his pension will be affected by it, even if the year that he earned the top raise is the last time he ever does an outstanding job again. If he continues to do just

enough to get by, he gets the reward every year after that anyway. Commissions, on the other hand, are reversible rewards. If an employee earns a particularly good commission one month, she gets it only once and then must earn it again next month.

6. The sixth rule about rewards is that they should be **durable.** Unfortunately, money tends not to be durable. A bonus is typically spent on a special item or trip or to pay a bill. A raise is usually figured into the family budget and the employee wonders how he ever paid his bills before he received it. On occasion, a unique employee will increase her savings or investments with part of a raise, which does make it more durable. A handwritten note is more durable than money. A promotion is durable. Money tends not to be. Think about the holiday turkey distributed to all employees. It does not follow any of the rules. If you spend $1,000 on turkeys, you have thrown $1,000 away. One $100 reward given publicly along with recognition for a job well done will do more for your department.

As a manager, your goal should be to develop rewards which follow most or all of the rules for effective rewards. You should note that the most effective rewards are not money. However, we must remind you again that money matters—just not in the way that most of us hope it will.

Research has shown us that providing rewards at or near the time that they are earned is best. Nonetheless, we pay our bills on a regular periodic basis and workers need to be paid on a periodic basis as well even though the pay period may not coincide with the performance. However, incentive pay and other rewards can easily be distributed when they are earned. Keep your pay ranges fair, based on market values, and adjusted to the cost of living. Then, use the money you have been spending on raises and turkeys to provide incentives directly tied to outstanding performance as it occurs or when goals are achieved.

Actually rewarding good performance is not the hardest part of the reward process. Measuring performance is more difficult.

PROVIDING PERFORMANCE FEEDBACK

The task of providing good performance feedback will be made much easier if the manager is developing and communicating challenging goals. Remember in Chapter 3 how we encouraged you to set measurable goals? This is where it pays off. Compare performance with the goals that were set. Even if specific goals are not used in your organization, there must be standards for performance. If not, how can the employee self-monitor and adjust his performance? If not, how can you monitor the performance of your direct reports and provide guidance and feedback on their performance?

Performance evaluation or appraisal should be a fairly simple process. Instead, it is one of the most difficult tasks of a manager. Usually, managers are required to complete a performance evaluation form. Different companies use different forms. Here are some steps to make the process easier.

Preparing the Performance Review

1. Throughout the review period, make notes whenever a critical incident occurs. A critical incident is any work behavior or performance that is out of the ordinary, good and bad. If someone finishes an assignment ahead of schedule, make a note of what occurred, date it, and put it into a file for that person. If a worker makes a mistake and does not correct it, make a note. At the end of the review period, these notes will be used to write the performance review. Remember that employees are entitled to see any file that you keep on them. Make sure that your notes are accurate and objective.
2. Make notes on day-to-day behavior that you notice. It is hard to remember everything and the day-to-day things are hardly ever noted during a performance evaluation. One bad incident should not cloud a year of productive service.
3. Make it a point to monitor workers' performance, objective measures of performance, and evidence of work performance (e.g., inspect repairs that have been made) as often as possible. Put yourself in a place where you can observe. Schedule time

to observe. It also helps if you work alongside an individual, at least on occasion. You will get a sense of the individual's job knowledge, as well as other aspects of performance. In addition, you can correct performance problems quickly—which is what we really care about anyway.

4. Review and give thought to the various factors that you must evaluate on the performance review form. You should consider the ratings before the time that you put them in writing.

5. List specific examples for each performance factor in the "Comments:" section. Check the appropriate statements listed under each category of ratings (i.e., "Below Standards," "Meets Standards," "Above Standards"). Check the correct rating for each performance factor last.

6. Do not ask the employee to fill out a copy of the performance review form. This is unnecessary. Completing this form is your job and seeing a copy of what the employee thinks will bias you. The employee has opinions and you need to hear those as you discuss each item. If the employee brings up information that you did not know or consider, you may decide to change the ratings. That is OK—if the change is accurate.

7. Discuss close calls with your peers and/or superior. It is important that all supervisors in the same department are giving similar ratings on similar performance. Help each other in order to increase the reliability of the review instrument.

Conducting the Performance Review Interview

1. Discuss the specific performance factors one at a time and in order.

2. Use specifics when you explain your ratings. Give examples and refer to measurements available.

3. Do not make general statements during the meeting like, "You are a hard worker." Instead, say, "You completed two extra projects." Don't say, "You don't try hard enough." Instead, say, "Your work was incomplete at least three times per week." Simple factual statements are not open for debate, but they *are* open for discussion.

4. Allow the employee to express opinions and concerns, but ask for examples. If an employee says, "You're not fair," ask for an example. Don't argue about a subjective opinion if an example cannot be given.
5. Keep the tone friendly, open, and honest by your use of words and body language. Monitor the employee's body language too. If you think there is a problem, take a few minutes to discuss it. If you treat a performance review as a secret and mysterious event, you will run into more problems. It is confidential, but not a CIA document. Honesty is always best even when you must deliver bad news. If you have been providing frequent feedback on performance, the employee knows that he is or is not performing up to standards.
6. At the end of the meeting, summarize the performance, emphasizing the negative feedback first and ending with the positive feedback.
7. Let the employee summarize his/her point of view.
8. If appropriate, discuss any action that will be taken next.
9. Give the employee a copy of the review and time to review your comments. Set up a second meeting if needed.
10. End the meeting on a positive note.

Building Optimism

We know that managers can build more optimistic workers and we know that more optimistic employees perform at a higher level. The method for doing this is not complicated, but it may fly in the face of strategies being used in many workplaces.

When someone does something well or when someone makes a mistake, we all attribute that success or failure to something. When a manager gives credit for successes directly to the worker it builds a feeling of optimism inside the employee. For example, if a direct report produces an excellent financial analysis, you should talk about that analysis as if the report did it alone and the success is due to his skills. If, on the other hand, a direct report does a poor financial analysis, the manager should talk about what the direct report can do differently, but also spread the blame a bit too. That might mean mentioning the fact that it was difficult to gather the data, the fact that the computer crashed halfway through the project, and that the format has just changed.

What is so different about this? It is a matter of how the credit or blame is placed. When we give all of the credit to the worker (instead of the new reporting system or the assistant), we are telling that employee that we believe that she is capable and successful on her own. When we spread the blame when things go wrong, we are allowing the employee to maintain their dignity and understand that other factors, besides their skill, also comes into play. This is quite different from "making people accept responsibility." Naturally, if someone makes lots of mistakes, you must do something about it. However, when a worker makes an occasional error, let them off the hook, so to speak and it will make them more optimistic and a better performer in the long run.

Are Your Direct Reports Motivated Yet?

Consider the people you supervise. After putting into practice all we've suggested, maybe they are still not motivated to do the work you need to have done. At least they know what you expect, understand the rewards for doing the work, and know what will happen if they do not. Now they can choose if they want to keep their jobs. The best things that can happen are that good employees stay and bad employees leave. The sooner the two of you make those things happen in a worker's career, the better off everyone will be. We all have choices which we must make about whether a job is right for us.

Fire employees who are not meeting performance standards after you have worked with them and done appropriate training. Nothing is less motivating to your employees than watching another's poor performance and feeling that their manager is powerless.

Do not try to fool employees into staying when a job is no longer motivating to them. Let us give you an example. Good administrative assistants are very hard to find. It is common for managers to discourage administrative assistants from applying for better jobs/promotional opportunities in companies because the manager does not want to lose the assistant. Usually, this involves giving her a large raise (often paying more than a secretary should make). In a year, when she is still dissatisfied, what have you gained? Good employees should be encouraged to move up instead of staying behind. A good administrative assistant may make an excellent customer service representative.

The bosses who most of us respect and who make us more effective employees are those who are supporters of our careers, coach us through difficult assignments, encourage us to try new things, respect our opinions, and tell us that they believe in us even when we are unsure about ourselves. They do not treat everyone the same. They appeal to our values and our personal needs. They reward us only when we have earned the reward and then they reward us appropriately using a variety of strategies.

EIGHT

Introducing and Implementing Change

A fundamental truth these days is that most organizations need to change far more often than ever before to succeed in the complex and unpredictable environments in which they operate. Effective organizations are those that can either proactively or reactively adapt to events occurring in their environments so that they can exploit opportunities, avoid threats, leverage their strengths, or overcome their weaknesses to maintain or enhance their performance. For many organizations, change is driven by their need to innovate to stay on the cutting edge. For those organizations, where innovation represents the foundation for their future success, the ability to change quickly and effectively is perhaps their most fundamental source of competitive advantage. We would expect that ability to be an inherent part of their "structural DNA." Unfortunately, we wouldn't always be correct in that expectation.

At the same time that managers are confronting ever-increasing pressures to change, another simple truth that they face is that their employees generally detest change. That is a psychological fact that must be understood right up front if managers are to have any realistic chance of introducing and implementing changes in their organizations. Because most people dislike change, they will often do everything in their power to resist it in the hopes of sabotaging it or hoping that it will go away. One reason why people resist change is fear of the unknown. The uncertainty that accompanies change is another reason for people's resistance. People who mistrust their supervisors or others in their organizations will resist change, as will people whose self-interest is at risk or, worse, whose very identities are threatened by changes. Finally, a less acute but equally important reason why people resist change is that they simply do not understand why it is occurring, especially when they do not view it as productive for their organization or work group. From a historical standpoint, change often meant danger to humans, so resisting change became a survival strategy. Unfortunately, we must manage people who still harbor the instinct to resist change.

We have organized this chapter around several issues that managers should consider when they confront the sometimes daunting task of change. To describe how to effectively overcome the challenges imposed by change, we have chosen one manager to use as example throughout this chapter. He isn't a famous champion of industry whom you have read about. While famous leaders have certainly been instrumental in bringing needed change to their respective companies and industries, we chose instead to present somebody who is a lot like us, to whom we can easily relate, and whose experiences and accomplishments might be within the reach of many more managers.

A SUCCESS STORY THAT YOU PROBABLY DO NOT KNOW

Eric Hoover was born and raised in a small town in northwestern Pennsylvania. As a youngster he was diagnosed with rheumatoid arthritis. In spite of a medical prognosis that included spending his life in a wheelchair, he proved his physicians wrong, overcame that condition, and built a thriving business enterprise from the ground up. A machinist by trade, he founded Excalibur Machine Company in 1998 to provide original equipment manufacturing, machining, and fabrication services for major manufacturing companies. That business has since expanded and evolved through a combination of acquisitions and natural business growth into a diversified company with annual revenues exceeding $40M and employing over 300 people in machining, metal fabrication, plastics tool-and-die making, construction, transportation, and sales.

That growth is all the more impressive given the significant decline in manufacturing in a region hit hard by overseas outsourcing. It wasn't easy, either. Hoover faced some major challenges when he integrated the operations of two plastics companies he acquired into his steel fabrication business. Those plastics companies were built on tool-and-die molding expertise, whereas Excalibur's core competence was in the area of metal machining. Those technologies are quite different, and the mind-sets of their respective skilled operators did not meld easily. However, Hoover has managed the change process most effectively.

Hoover's success as an entrepreneur was recognized in 2006 with his selection as the U.S. Small Business Administration's National Small Business Person of the Year, an award presented to him during a Washington, DC, ceremony attended by President George W. Bush. His accomplishments are quite a feat and should serve as an inspiration to all of us. He has always recognized the need for change, and attributes his success largely to his ability to recognize opportunities and adapt to them. As a visionary leader with a strong orientation toward the future, he planned for change from the beginning, establishing ten-year outlooks for Excalibur during the company's infancy that pushed him to grow his business aggressively. He is a modest, unassuming man who has managed to do some extraordinary things during his life.

HOW TO KNOW WHEN CHANGE IS NEEDED

This is the fundamental issue, to be sure. Sometimes it arises from one's recognition of a performance gap—that is, a difference between actual and desired levels of performance. Although often the first signal of the need for change, a performance gap is typically unnoticed until it becomes a problem, which unfortunately is often too late. We tend to ignore slight differences between our expected and attained outcomes, attributing them to circumstances beyond our control, external conditions that will shift before too long, random fluctuations or "noise" (everyday annoyances and disturbances) in our environments. One way managers can identify performance gaps more quickly is through more careful and more frequent attention to details, and a more thorough analysis of why and how certain outcomes are attained. That prescription is easily given but seldom serves as a cure because performance gaps often cause managers to fall into the trap of "threat rigidity" where they revert to a small set of previously successful strategies, including avoidance, overreaction, and dealing with symptoms rather than identifying the root causes for undesired performance. By exhibiting those behaviors, managers frequently enter into a downward spiral of overly sensitive reactions to every little nuance, resulting in actions that only make matters worse.

Even if managers can deal effectively with change when confronted with performance gaps, those instances of change represent sporadic responses even in the best cases. A more effective way of dealing with the need for change is to get out in front and drive it yourself before it becomes a problem. By dealing with change proactively, you can manage it rather than allowing it to manage you. Eric Hoover is quick to state that "we drive change; it doesn't drive us." Communicating that message is absolutely essential for managers who wish to deal with change before they notice performance gaps. Unless everybody hears that message, managers will be walking a tightrope without benefit of a net. As a leader, Hoover takes every opportunity to not only communicate that message but also to ensure that everybody understands that change is the way of life that will ensure their company's success as it has done in the past, and will guarantee its (and their) continued growth and prosperity. To him, proactive change represents the easiest way to grow. "You need to be constantly reinventing yourself," he says, noting that the only way to do so is to have everybody on board with that philosophy. He enjoys getting people excited about change because it keeps everybody engaged in thinking about a future that is better than today.

Hoover believes that if his company isn't in the process of changing to become better, he is negligent because he is effectively allowing it to become worse. Accordingly, he believes in the principle of continuous improvement. He also understands that continuous improvement is a process, not an outcome. Under the drive to continuously improve, his company seldom actually "finishes the job." In his view, if a continuous improvement goal is implemented 100 percent, it is a sign that there isn't enough on people's plates to keep them busy. So how does Eric know that change is needed? He operates under the assumption that it is needed on a continual basis and never second guesses himself.

Change can take many forms. As we have already said, some changes are externally induced—changes in markets, competitors, societal norms, regulations, and the like. Some changes are internally generated—changes to processes or procedures, products, and services. Internal changes often fall under the classification of innovations. Some innovations represent incremental advances in a technology family whereas some represent radical departures from existing technology. The former are less risky but the latter provide opportunities to reinvent industries and markets. Hoover recognizes that, and knows that continuous improvement changes must not be allowed to become the sole focus. If they do, the organization stands an excellent chance of missing the next seismic shift in technology.

Sometimes managers can't envision or accept the need for innovative change by themselves, and Hoover is no exception. Accordingly, he places a high value on change agents. Change agents are those people who have the unique ability to recognize opportunities or threats and thus the need for change in advance of others, and the wherewithal to help get it started and carried out. They can come from any part of the organization, and exist at any hierarchical level.

Hoover considers every one of his employees as possible change agents, and especially those who have been with him the longest and who have experienced the company's success over time. Because initiating and assuming the responsibility for managing change can be asking a lot from a single person, he understands the different roles that people fulfill as change agents. Some act as *inventors*, or the architects of change. They develop creative ideas but often don't know how to win support for them. Some serve as *idea champions;* those people believe in the ideas of inventors, can visualize the benefits, and understand the organizational processes sufficiently to help initiate the change effort. *Sponsors* are usually people who are highly respected in an organization. Some people take the role of sponsor, and remove barriers that might confront change agents. Those people are usually, but not always, mid- or high-level managers. Finally, some perform as *critics*, providing hard-nosed reality checks and playing the Devil's advocate with inventors to help them sharpen their ideas and develop their logic to the fullest. Knowing who can function in those various change agent roles provides Hoover with an enormous reservoir of talent that can be brought to bear on just about any type of change issue. Motivated people make the best change agents, and Hoover says "we keep motivated people—we will train them—we care about the people who are going to make us better and help us grow."

HOW TO GET CHANGE STARTED

This is an even more intimidating issue for many managers, because it implies commitment to a process with an uncertain outcome. Getting started involves planning. The first action that is required is to communicate that change is on your radar. Discuss what changes you are considering with people individually and collectively. Solicit their feedback early, before doing any real formal planning for change. In that way, people will start to get used to the idea well before it is thrust upon them. To use this technique effectively, however, there must be a climate of mutual trust and respect, and the leader's vision must be well understood. Eric Hoover makes himself visible to all of his employees, and keeps lines of communication open so that they can speak their minds to him anytime and anywhere—especially when he is pondering changes. He considers it imperative to make people comfortable so that they will contribute their honest opinions during the process. By behaving in such a manner, he signals to them that his commitment and support of them is genuine.

Hoover never passes up an opportunity to communicate with his employees. He uses multiple media to do so, including an internal company newsletter, regular management meetings, and a series of what he calls "lunch meetings"—even if they are scheduled in the middle of the night. Those meetings are conducted once a month at each of his four facilities for all three shifts, concentrated in a single week. He usually distributes an agenda for the informational part of those meetings, particularly when he is announcing something new. However, he is usually more interested in asking questions and listening to his peoples' responses. He is one of those managers who actually listen to what people say, not because it makes employees feel good but because they have a lot to contribute. He admits that new employees who had formerly worked for companies that he had acquired were initially hesitant to say anything during those sessions, and that he needed to establish trust and rapport with them. That takes time, and managers must recognize that fact. Open and honest communication is the logical first step.

Another action that has proven to be effective in planning for change is to encourage people to be active participants from the beginning of the change process. Involving people early and often makes them an integral part of the planning process and is probably the single most important thing that managers can do to ensure the success of change. Educate your people about the need for change and involve them actively in the planning and implementation process. Doing so will not only reduce their natural resistance to change, it will also provide managers with an excellent source of ideas, some very creative, that can be used both in the present and the future. It has been demonstrated that when people are participants in any process, they soon shift from the category of "involved" to the category of "committed." If they are heard, and especially if their ideas are used, they will develop psychological ownership of the change—which is a powerful state of mind and one which increases the chances of successful change enormously.

Brainstorming is a tool that has proven to be extremely valuable in getting people to open up and contribute their thoughts to discussions about change. Hoover is a proponent of brainstorming, and he knows that when people are first exposed to that process they need to be encouraged to contribute. Described by Hoover as "dragging ideas" out of people at first, he knows that if he establishes a climate of trust and mutual respect, they will soon get used to it and look forward to it as an opportunity to show off what they can bring to the table. Even when he has a pretty good idea about what kind of changes need to be made, Hoover generally prefers to lay out the situation, rather than his own approach toward its solution, thereby allowing his people to create a plan for change. More often than not, he is pleased with what they devise.

Managers frequently need to be internal sales people. Selling change can be a tough task, but if done correctly it can also produce excellent results. Hoover found himself in that position when he realized that he had to convince his newly acquired tool-and-die people that they would be performing less work for OEMs (original-equipment manufacturers) than they had in the past. In fact, all of their business had previously been OEM related. He had to sell them on the advantages of shifting their expertise to manufacturing fixtures for the machining business. Although they were resistant, he convinced them that what they needed to do was not all that different from what they had been doing throughout their careers—that they were still mold builders, but that the customers for their molds were now internal and they would be helping to improve the manufacturing process that would produce products for OEMs, thus improving the entire organization. The concept that Hoover used enabled his mold builders to preserve their core identity while requiring them to modify slightly their thinking about who their customers were. It wasn't just the mold builders that had to be sold. It was everybody who had been affiliated with those acquired plastics companies, management as well as rank-and-file workers. Otherwise, the desired change (in this case, integrating formerly autonomous businesses into a single efficient company) would have been a failure.

Another tool that is useful in structuring people's participation in the change process is a force-field analysis. Although that might sound like something from Star Trek, it is really a simple but effective way to ensure that all factors are considered during planning for change. In a force-field analysis, all of the forces for and against a change are listed in separate lists, with the goal of identifying relatively equal numbers of both. Those sets of forces are called driving and restraining forces, respectively. By delineating those forces, managers are less likely to overlook them, and far less likely to fall victim to them.

For example, consider a common change: the adoption of a new information system. As managers, it is easy for us to see the advantages of such a change—better access to data, updated reporting procedures, increased organizational flexibility, a better way to communicate instantly with valued customers and suppliers, and enhanced organizational efficiency. Now, try to find a restraining force to accompany each of the driving forces—for example, fear of losing one's position in the information chain, anxiety related to having to learn a new system, changing internal procedures and upsetting established routines, initial expense, training requirements, and the initial drop in performance that accompanies anything new. After all of the forces have been considered simultaneously, participants can devise ways of dealing with the resisting forces to ensure that they don't neutralize or, worse, overwhelm the driving forces.

Although we believe that healthy internal competition has its place, one thing that Hoover resists doing is setting up "friendly" competition between various units in his company. Because he needs his people to flow from group to group, he doesn't want them to feel attached to any particular unit. When organizations require such flexibility, avoiding internal competition is appropriate. Mixing people up often leads to freer communications. On one occasion, Hoover physically removed a wall in one of his buildings that had separated two departments—computer programming and engineering—so that they would communicate more freely. The result? Far more effective and efficient interaction.

ENSURING THAT CHANGE GETS IMPLEMENTED SUCCESSFULLY

Implementation is by far the most difficult part of the change process. It involves action rather than words, and it requires the effort of people who might still be resistant to the change. After all of the planning, you need to take action and get it accomplished. Implementation is often where people's resistance to change is most prominently on display, and the business world is filled with examples of wonderful plans that never saw the light of day because they simply could not be implemented. To increase the chances of implementation success, one important thing to do is to make implementation an integral part of the planning process itself—not an afterthought. We must emphasize that implementation difficulties should never be allowed to undercut good ideas. However, certain organizational realities must be considered during planning for change. For example, if your company has built its reputation on high quality, differentiated products, and superb customer service, it will be very difficult to implement changes designed to enter low-end markets with standard products. Such a change would cause confusion right at the core identity of the company, and would be likely to fail because of its inconsistency with a strong company culture and its norms and values.

In addition to the advice we offer above for maximizing communication and participation, we offer several additional suggestions for improving the chances for successful implementation. One is to anticipate mistakes and allow them to happen. They are a necessary part of the change process. Hoover knew that his organization was going to make some mistakes when he integrated elements of newly acquired companies into the organizational structure of Excalibur, and it did. However, rather than punishing the guilty, he viewed those mistakes as a relatively inexpensive "college education," as he described it, and discussed what happened with the responsible parties to make sure that they didn't make those same mistakes again. By handling mistakes as an opportunity to learn, they become constructive.

Another thing that managers can do is to force people with different perspectives to work together with a superordinate goal in mind. A superordinate goal is one that individuals or single departments cannot achieve by themselves. Instead, it requires that everyone work together. Hoover established some challenging superordinate goals when he forced three groups of people to figure out how to function together—steel machinists and two groups of plastics tool-and-die mold builders who had always competed against each other. Success came when they focused on their similarities and stopped emphasizing their differences. As Hoover put it, "at the end of the day, they all put chips on the floor."

When managers require people to work together to achieve change, it is inevitable that at some point they will have to be arbiters, sometimes choosing one side or perhaps even a compromise. Hoover notes that such instances are rare in his company, but because his people work in a climate of mutual trust, they accept his decisions because they recognize that he always strives to be fair. He will take the time to explain his decision, emphasize that there are no "losers," and reassure people that their position might prevail the next time. On one occasion, he literally flipped a coin in full view of two parties to decide between their respective ideas because each had merit and he could not identify a clear winner!

When managers empower people, they don't simply *allow* them to make decisions and implement them—they *expect* them to do so and hold them accountable. They avoid micromanaging people and they allow individual discretion from people who have demonstrated their ability to use it effectively. One way for a manager to empower people and have them work together is for managers to deliberately disassociate themselves from discussions of change implementation and allow a solution to emerge bottom-up. Hoover has deliberately missed meetings about change so that the other participants have to get along without him. By doing so, he is convinced that he is building an organization that can function without him and yet still adhere to his ideals about change, avoiding complacency and stagnation.

Empowerment has enormous potential as an instrument of change. Hoover recently allowed a general manager at one of his plants to resign without replacing him. Instead, he allowed the three members of the existing management team who had reported to that general manager to "step up" and manage their plant together. They were good people who had been well trained. So far, that arrangement is working well and, in our view, it is a wonderful example of empowerment.

Forcing people to work together is one way to get them to do so, but it sometimes resembles the stick of the carrot-and-stick approach. The carrot also has great potential for success. In short, incentives and encouragement are useful. For example, Hoover's introduction of something new for his industry—a gain sharing plan—encouraged his people to work together because of the combined effects of the financial incentives. As a result of their efforts in 2006, every employee received $0.44/hr times the number of hours worked, regardless of their position, pay rate, or education, from Hoover, himself, down to the lowest-level employee. This was *after* he made some charitable contributions, set aside internal growth funds, and budgeted for research and development expenses. He also emphasizes to his employees that their ability to change the company for the better has allowed him to implement a health plan and a wellness plan where he pays 100 percent of the costs of premiums for all of his employees and their families. By aligning his employees' incentives with the mandate to continuously change his company, implementation of changes is facilitated.

Successful change implementation requires visible and genuine top management commitment, appropriate education, constant communication, and active participation of those who will carry out and/or be affected by the changes. If managers follow those prescriptions, and provide the necessary facilitation and support, they will not have to resort to tactics that seldom work effectively—namely, negotiation, manipulation, or coercion—except in rare circumstances.

Organizations that create a culture that embraces change can benefit far more from the creativity of their people than those that do not, enjoying a constantly replenished source of innovative ideas. They are also able to achieve greater leverage from their core competencies, or their sets of integrated and harmonized capabilities that distinguish them from other organizations and provide the basis of their competitive advantage. How? By refreshing those competencies through dynamic renewal, ensuring that they are never allowed to become core rigidities. The "evil twin" of core competencies, core rigidities constrain creative, future-oriented, productive changes because they result from an obsessive focus on the present and past successes without any consideration of what is needed to pursue future opportunities.

As Hoover says, "It's all about the people." Treat them with respect, make sure that they understand the need for change, get them involved early and often in the change process, empower them to implement changes, and reward them accordingly. In that way, a simple equation emerges:

Innovative leadership + employees open to change + effective rewards = successful change

NINE

Understanding and Dealing with Competitors

Dealing with competitors is something that affects most managers, either directly or indirectly, even if they do not participate actively in the crafting of their organizations' strategies. Although competitive analysis is an integral part of the strategy-making process, and top managers spend considerable time and resources doing just that, it is also imperative that managers at all levels and in all functions understand their roles in handling competitors. As a practical matter, relatively few managers actually participate in *formulating* corporate- or business-level strategies, but most managers play important parts in *implementing* those strategies. Implementation is where the rubber meets the road, so to speak, and it is always— repeat, always—the weak link in the process of strategic management. Why? Because implementation requires action based on a thoughtful and accurate assessment of one's competitive situation.

Strategic management is fundamentally about attaining, maintaining, and enhancing competitive advantage, which is an edge over industry rivals. Competitive advantage is measured in relative terms; that is, only in comparison to one's competitors. It is not absolute, it is not a birthright, and it is surely not cast in stone. Because competitive advantage is relative rather than absolute, it can come and go, so an imperative of effective management is to sustain competitive advantage as long as possible. Ask managers which task is more difficult—achieving competitive advantage or maintaining it. Most will answer that getting to the top of the hill is far easier than staying there. Once you have achieved some measure of success, you might as well wear a large target on your back. Your competitors will come after you with relentless energy and the full power of their resources. Just think about college football. Although we like to dream about our beloved alma maters competing for the national championship on an annual basis, that does not occur. Few teams can remain in the top tier for more than a few years, let alone actually win a championship.

In the business world, competitors gain and lose position, technological advantages arise and vanish with startling rapidity, and customer preferences can shift at the drop of a hat. Formidable companies can lose their footing and slip into disastrous circumstances. Consider the example of IBM, which for years had an enormous competitive advantage in office computing based on its mainframe technology and legendary field service capabilities. Rather than simply give up and settle in as also-rans, many of IBM's traditional competitors, as well as some new players in the market, shifted their technological emphasis in another direction in the mid- to late-1980s. IBM then saw its edge vanish with the rise of distributed desktop computing. After a painful several years during which the company came dangerously close to irrelevance and financial ruin, it made a comeback in the early- to mid-1990s with a new emphasis on information systems solutions, and regained much of its former luster.

The edge that organizations need in order to have some competitive advantage can be the result of many attributes of their products or services; for example, low cost, high quality, excellent features, unique functionality, location or convenience, or some combination thereof. Those attributes create superior value, which is determined solely by customers. Again, however, competitors can create value in different ways that are sometimes superior to others. That is why managers need to truly understand their specific competitors and devise ways to deal with them.

We recommend a five-step process for managers to deal with competitors:

- Step 1: Scan and evaluate your competitive environment
- Step 2: Identify your competitors
- Step 3: Categorize your competitors
- Step 4: Analyze your competitors
- Step 5: Devise actions to compete effectively

STEP 1: SCAN AND EVALUATE YOUR COMPETITIVE ENVIRONMENT

The only way to keep up with your competitors is through constant environmental scanning. By that, we mean gathering information from outside of the organization for analysis. By scanning the organization's environment, managers can determine their competitors' positions and the competitive moves that they are likely to make to maintain or enhance their own competitive advantage. Which managers should be involved in environmental scanning? All managers. Even if you do not deal directly with competitors, you probably interact with other managers in other organizations who can be a valuable source of information about your competitors.

Sales managers, of course, should be directly attuned to competitors—or else they won't be sales managers for long. Likewise, marketing managers need to focus their attention directly on competitors if they are to develop effective marketing strategies. Although everybody recognizes the obvious importance of sales and marketing managers in assessing the competition, the most effective organizations make use of many more managers in the process.

For example, purchasing managers interact with suppliers on a daily basis. Don't those suppliers also provide products or services to your competitors? Of course they do, so they are an excellent source of information concerning what your competitors are up to. Human resource managers deal with the labor market, so they are frequently in contact with potential hires who might currently or formerly be employed by your competitors. Manufacturing and operations managers communicate with experts in information technology and production processes, who are very likely to provide similar services to your competitors. Research and development managers confront the same or similar technological changes as your competitors, and are likely to talk frequently with representatives of your competitors as a matter of professional interaction. Financial analysts can identify the financial ups and downs of your competitors, which can be early signals about their future behavior. And so on.

In this way, even though any one manager lacks the complete picture, the composite of a number of managers together should provide a pretty good glimpse into what competitors are doing and how well they are doing it. If your organization isn't piecing those snippets of information together in any systematic way, you can surely talk to other managers and start to do so yourself.

The information obtained from environmental scanning is instrumental in the construction of a comprehensive situation analysis on which to devise alternative competitive approaches. You might have heard a situation analysis called a SWOT analysis—short for **S**trengths, **W**eaknesses, **O**pportunities, and **T**hreats. A SWOT analysis should be performed for every unique competitive situation that an organization confronts. Strengths and weaknesses are internal attributes of the organization that are largely within management's control, while opportunities and threats are external factors over which organizations seldom have any control or influence.

For every competitive situation, managers should make a list of the relevant organizational strengths possessed and weaknesses that will be exposed, as well as the opportunities presented and the threats anticipated. Based on how the internal and external factors line up, managers can determine ways to deal with the competition. For example, if a competitive situation is largely opportunistic and plays into your strengths, the prescription is easy—marshal your resources and generate actions that utilize your strengths to exploit opportunities before your competitors do. If a situation is far more threatening and is likely to uncover your weaknesses, the recommended advice is simple—minimize your weaknesses by avoiding threats and quickly get out of the way.

Unfortunately, competitive situations seldom fit into one of those two categories. The overwhelming majority fall into competitive "gray areas." If a situation presents opportunities but points more toward your weaknesses, you can do several things, including generating actions to exploit those opportunities by overcoming your weaknesses and turning them into strengths. For example, you might have a customer tell you that he/she likes the features of your products, and that he/she would purchase more products from you if you switched to a slightly different technology. If you lack sufficient expertise in that technology, you could decide to establish an extensive training program for your employees to provide them with the requisite technological education and training, or you could decide to immediately hire experts in that technology and have them start to develop the new products that your customers desire.

Alternatively, you could make the difficult call and choose not to pursue that particular opportunity, returning to battle another day. Referring to the example above, you might choose to forego an attempt to satisfy that immediate customer need because it might simply require the dedication of too many resources, and focus instead on developing future products so superior to your competitors' that your customer will overcome its fondness for the other technology and end up buying more of your products anyway. If a situation appears threatening but your strengths can be brought to bear directly on it, one approach would be to implement actions that use those strengths to overcome the threats head-on, attempting to turn them into opportunities.

For example, if some of your clients threaten to take their accounting business to a competitor because you don't have the capacity to provide them with timely service, you could decide to hire a team of accountants, even in a labor market where you know that you will have to overpay them for their expertise, or you might decide to outsource your work even though you would have to pay even more for accounting services, just to keep your clients with the expectation that you could eventually recoup the additional expenses that you would incur. Competitive frontal assaults such as that can obviously be risky, so another approach would be to leverage your strengths and avoid threats directly by working around them. Using the example above, you could begin to prospect for new clients that would appreciate the excellent accounting expertise that you offer, and would therefore be less demanding about the timeliness of the delivery of those services.

It should be apparent by now that there are few hard and fast rules, but a variety of different competitive alternatives that all rest on a solid understanding of your own capabilities and factors in your environment—especially your competitors.

STEP 2: IDENTIFY YOUR COMPETITORS

Although this seems like a no-brainer, you would be surprised by how many companies possess huge blind spots in identifying who their competitors are and, perhaps more importantly, who their competitors will be in the near future. Most managers can, of course, rattle off the names of their most salient competitors, and in some industries the number of competitors is bounded and well known (e.g., the automobile industry). Because industry barriers are constantly shifting, managers should take a broader perspective on what constitutes a competitor. A number of years ago, a relatively new Disney CEO, Michael Eisner, determined that his company was losing an opportunity to expand its theme park business by focusing its attention on large amusement parks in the United States. Eisner convinced his top managers that the Disney theme park business didn't compete in the amusement park industry, it competed in the vacation industry. That not-so-subtle change in focus unlocked tremendous opportunities to grow, especially in central Florida. As a consequence of that restatement of its industry, however, Disney now faced considerably more competitors than before; specifically, any first-rate company in the family vacation business.

The misidentification of competitors often results from our assumptions based on past experience, and those assumptions can be dangerous. One example of this is Caterpillar's failure to identify Komatsu as a viable competitor, based in large part on the faulty assumption that Caterpillar enjoyed a large quality advantage (which in fact had narrowed considerably in a few short years) that allowed the company to command price premiums for its heavy construction machinery. The fact was that Komatsu's heavy equipment had become nearly as good as Caterpillar's and was priced substantially lower, thereby producing a better price/performance ratio resulting in greater value that customers recognized and appreciated.

Another example is Xerox's initial dismissal of Canon copiers as viable competitive threats, despite evidence that customers approved of them. Yet another is CBS's failure to identify Fox's program offerings in the late 1980s and early 1990s as viable prime-time entertainment. After all, who in the world would watch *The Simpsons, Married...with Children,* or *Beverly Hills, 90210?* A final example of poorly identifying a potential competitor is the way that the major television news networks virtually ignored nascent CNN, until the events of the Persian Gulf War unfolded in mid-1990 and CNN's on-scene correspondents provided their network with a virtual lock on credible news from the region. Even when the major networks mobilized their teams, CNN maintained its position as the network to watch, and the company solidified market share that it has never relinquished, much to the detriment of its long-established competitors.

The pivotal question that managers need to ask themselves to properly identify their competitors is "what is my industry?" because the answer to that question will help them identify competitors earlier in the game. The trend in today's business climate is to define one's industry more broadly, thereby allowing for greater business opportunities. The Disney example discussed above represents that way of thinking, as do several others: soft drink companies have expanded broadly into just about all nonalcoholic beverages; many computer companies now offer information system solutions instead of just computers; toy companies now manufacture and sell other children's products including bedroom and playroom furniture and educational games; and photocopier companies (i.e., Xerox) and photographic companies (i.e., Kodak) now compete against each other in the imaging systems industry. Identifying new competitors is essential to the success of those companies.

Additionally, companies that can anticipate changes in their industries are in a position to devise ways to deal with them in advance of actual competition. For example, a number of life insurance companies recognized the 1999 repeal of the Glass-Steagall Act of 1933 (which had put restrictions on the activities of banks to limit their power as financial conglomerates) as an opportunity to compete more broadly in financial services, and started positioning themselves to face new competitors well prior to its passage.

STEP 3: CATEGORIZE YOUR COMPETITORS

After you have identified your competitors, you should classify them individually so that you can gain greater insight to their respective objectives and strategies. By doing so, you can determine whether your competitors pose an immediate, direct threat to your business, or whether they compete with you more indirectly. We recommend using the following set of factors: competitive scope, strategic intent, competitive position and situation, strategic posture, and broad strategy. That list might sound complicated, but it is really pretty straightforward, and using those factors will result in a comprehensive examination of the major competitive elements of each of your competitors.

Competitive scope refers to the extent of your competitors' competitive aspirations—i.e., global, national, regional, or local.

Strategic intent concerns your competitors' immediate major objectives in the marketplace—i.e., growth, survival, maintaining present position, desire to lead, content to follower, defense of a narrow market niche, etc.

Competitive position and situation indicates your competitors' current strength and trends in that strength in the recent past— strong and getting stronger, weak and becoming weaker, strong but slipping, or weak but rising.

Strategic posture involves whether your competitor is aggressive or defensive, and risk-taking or conservative.

Broad strategy has to do with whether your competitors are competing primarily on the basis of low price, differentiation (i.e., unique products, services, or features), or overall best value.

List each of your competitors and categorize them on those factors. Then categorize your own company. Do you see the similarities and differences? Based on your categorization, at this point you should be confident that you have sufficient information on which to base a reasonable expectation of the moves that your competitors are likely to make. You can start to see whether and how those competitors will be competing directly or indirectly with you.

STEP 4: ANALYZE YOUR COMPETITORS

You have now collected a lot of valuable information about your competitors, but much of it is still likely to be unorganized and "raw." Now you need to put it in an organized framework so that you can devise specific competitive moves to beat or counter their competitive actions.

A competitive strength assessment is a powerful tool that any manager can develop and use. It will reveal to you the strength of your competitive position and the relative strength of the competitive position of each of the specific competitors you have identified throughout this process. It takes a little time to put together, but that effort will be rewarded many times over. Once you have developed the competitive strength assessment, you will be able to modify it periodically or as the situation changes with reasonably little effort. Wouldn't you prefer to know about your specific competitors so that you can target your resources for maximum impact, rather than to allocate your resources toward some global, nonspecific objective known only as "the competition"?

The competitive strength assessment requires that managers consider not only their specific competitors, but also important features of their industries. Those features are called *key success factors*. For every industry, a few factors are critical for all companies that wish to compete successfully, and they therefore will frame the success or failure of all competitors. Think of them as the table stakes, or ante, required to get into a card game. Key success factors vary by industry. For example, in the fast-food industry the key success factors are:

- Speed of service
- Convenience/location
- Taste
- Quality
- Variety
- Value

Companies that perform well on those factors might not lead the industry in performance, but they will at least have the opportunity to achieve some competitive advantage. Companies that perform poorly on a single one, let alone several, of those factors are probably doomed to fail. Most managers have a very good idea of the handful of key success factors that govern their industries.

To begin to construct your competitive strength assessment, list your industry's key success factors vertically on a spreadsheet or a sheet of paper. We cannot think of any industry with more than a dozen or so that need to be considered. Then, list your company and your most important competitors horizontally across the top of the spreadsheet or your paper. Once you have done that, the real work begins.

Using a convenient scale (we recommend 1–5), rate your company and each of your competitors on every one of the industry key success factors. Be brutally honest. You should include assessments of your respective strengths made by your mutual customers, who will usually be more than happy to provide that information so that they receive better products and services. Using a variety of tools including focus groups, product samples, and detailed conversations, you can find out what your customers think about your products and your competitors' products. Are your customers' needs being met, and if so by which companies? What would make products more appealing to them? What services would they like to see improved? What don't they like about your company and your competitors? Harley-Davidson used these techniques successfully when the company devised a new marketing strategy that provided it with the major boost it needed to regain its dominant position in the U.S. motorcycle market.

Add up the scores and you will get an indication of how everybody stacks up relative to each other. Refer to Table 9.1 for an example. It illustrates an imaginary industry with the seven key success factors indicated. Note that in this example, your company is ranked second to Competitor X, and just ahead of Competitor Z. Competitor Y appears to be bringing up the rear.

You can take a deep breath at this point, but you aren't done. You have merely completed the first pass through your data and you only have a rough idea about what it means. If companies have very close scores, you would be rash to rate one ahead of another because small differences at this point are virtually meaningless.

Now, perform a weighted competitive strength assessment. To do so, apply weights to the key success factors. For example, if your industry key success factors include product reliability and manufacturing efficiency, and they are of about equal importance, they should be assigned the same weight. If both of those factors are less important than, say, customer service, and you deem customer service to be twice as important, then assign it a weight commensurate with that assessment. After you have weighted all of the key success factors, then multiply those rates by the ratings you

Table 9.1   Unweighted Competitive Strength Assessment

Key Success Factors	Your Company	Competitor X	Competitor Y	Competitor Z
Breadth of product line	4	4	3	5
Customer service	3	5	1	2
Distributor network	2	5	4	3
Efficient manufacturing	5	2	5	3
New product development time	5	3	1	2
Product reliability	2	4	2	4
Quality	3	3	1	4
Total	**24**	**26**	**17**	**23**
Rank	**2**	**1**	**4**	**3**

assigned to each company, and add the results again. Compare each competitor's score and don't be surprised if a different picture emerges.

Refer to Table 9.2. Note that now your company ranks *third*, following Competitor X, which looks even stronger, and Competitor Z, which has leapfrogged you. How did that happen? Simple. Although the rankings of each company on the key success factor are unchanged, both of those companies scored higher than yours on criteria that you judge to be more important; i.e., key success factors that you weighted more heavily. That is not unusual, by the way.

Are you through yet? Hardly, and we wouldn't bet our professional reputations on that assessment just yet. We recommend at this point that you perform a sensitivity analysis. That analysis will reveal to you just how sensitive your assessment is to minor fluctuations in your ratings. Go back through and reevaluate each rating. Did you perhaps inflate some, and undervalue others? Make some minor adjustments if they seem reasonable—we repeat, *minor* adjustments, or "tweaks." It is pointless to make major changes, because if you lack confidence in your ratings in the first place, you haven't accomplished the previous steps with any degree of validity. After you have made those minor changes, run the numbers of the weighted assessment again. Observe your results.

Table 9.2 Weighted Competitive Strength Assessment

Key Success Factors	Weight	Your Company	Comp. X	Comp. Y	Comp. Z
Breadth of product line	2	4 (8)	4 (8)	3 (6)	5 (10)
Customer service	3	3 (9)	5 (15)	1 (3)	2 (6)
Distributor network	3	2 (6)	5 (15)	4 (12)	3 (9)
Efficient manufacturing	1	5 (5)	2 (2)	5 (5)	3 (3)
New product development time	1	5 (5)	3 (3)	1 (1)	2 (2)
Product reliability	2	2 (4)	4 (8)	2 (4)	4 (8)
Quality	3	3 (9)	3 (9)	1 (3)	4 (12)
Total		**46**	**60**	**34**	**50**
Rank		**3**	**1**	**4**	**2**

If you wish, make minor adjustments to the weights themselves and recalculate. If you get virtually the same result each time—that is, if each competitor ranks the same relative to all of the others—then your assessment is robust. Good! You have the basis for devising specific credible actions to compete with each of your rivals. If your results shift each time, then your assessment is sensitive, and you cannot conclude much about the relative strengths of your competitors or how you stack up against them. More work is needed to collect accurate information about your competitors and, perhaps, your own company.

Would you like to look into the future? You can analyze your competitors' future competitive strength if you make one important modification to the competitive strength assessment: instead of using your industry's key success factors, identify and use your industry's *driving forces* instead. Driving forces are those forces that are starting to drive an industry to change. Although they have not achieved competitive parity with key success factors at present, they surely will in the immediate future, and will determine the fate of competitors in the next several years. By substituting those driving forces in the assessment, you can glimpse into the future and determine how your competitors will be likely to stack up tomorrow. Returning to our example of the fast-food industry, driving forces include such things as:

- Health-conscious choices
- Décor and ambience
- Creative (or even gourmet) menu options

STEP 5: DEVISE ACTIONS TO COMPETE EFFECTIVELY

By now, you can probably guess that we recommend different approaches to dealing with each of your competitors. A "one size fits all" strategy really won't fit anything. Every one of your competitors has soft spots that should become clear in your competitive strength assessment.

If a specific competitor is vulnerable to price competition, then a viable option for you is to compete with it on that basis, provided that is one of your strengths. You must educate your customers to the fact that your products or services are every bit as good as those of that specific competitor, only priced lower. A low-price strategy, however, cannot be sustained indefinitely, especially against a larger competitor. You will need to devise other ways to differentiate your company in the mind of your customer. There can be only one low-price leader at a time, and if you attempt to compete on that basis but you cannot be "the" low price leader, you are not going to achieve much success, because there are usually no points for second place. Just ask Kmart executives what happened to their company when they tried to go head-to-head with Wal-Mart in the 1990s.

Most companies differentiate themselves against their specific competitors on the basis of other attributes. Again, turn to your competitive strength assessment and look for areas in which you are strong and one or more competitors are weak, especially if those key success factors are weighted more heavily. Devise actions to emphasize those differences in the minds of your customers. Where your company comes up short, initiate actions to bolster your shortcomings or, alternatively, avoid those competitors directly and compete with others that are less powerful. Competing on the basis of differentiation requires that you provide product or service attributes that are unmatched by your rivals and valued for their uniqueness by discriminating customers. Choose your battles carefully—you simply cannot compete with everybody, in every market segment, with equal fervor, all of the time. Few organizations possess the resources to sustain broad-based competitive campaigns against all comers. If yours does, then fortune has smiled upon you.

Another way to compete is through an overall best value strategy, one that is more difficult to execute but that is becoming more common in many industries, including consumer electronics and personal computers. The reason that it is difficult is that it requires your company to continually lower costs *and* increase differentiation, with the result being more value for your customer—i.e., providing products or services that have superior price/performance ratios. To be successful, it is imperative that you know how your competitors achieve leverage from their strengths and minimize their weaknesses, because they will be attempting to compete in much the same way that you are. You simply cannot afford to fall victim to another common blind spot in competitor analysis—over-emphasizing your competitors' visible attributes, or *what* they do, at the expense of really digging and finding out *how* they do what they do. You need to lift up the hood and get inside their "engines."

Another way of dealing with your competitors is to follow the old adage "if you can't beat 'em, join 'em." After all, partnering with a competitor can enable your organizations to achieve some objective jointly that neither of you could hope to achieve on your own. Such a hybrid model is called "co-opetition"[1] because it combines elements of cooperation and competition. The idea is for two (or more) companies to work together to achieve a common goal. Cooperative competition is aimed at increasing the size of the pie as opposed to worrying about the size of your slice, with the result that you will of course enjoy a bigger slice even if others do as well. In that sense, co-opetition is unlike the formation of a cartel or other structure designed to limit competition. Instead of slugging it out with powerful competitors, smaller companies can unite with other similar companies, most appropriately those with complementary capabilities, to provide a formidable competitive front and to promote their industry so that it grows, which benefits everybody.

Examples of co-opetition have been evident in the computer industry for years, where alliances between hardware and software firms in particular (e.g., Apple and Microsoft) have resulted in the development of creative new products and even new markets. Further, Apple's entry in the mobile communications industry, the iPhone, is supported by the company's partnership with an established competitor in that industry, AT&T Mobility. Apple produces multimedia Internet-enabled mobile phones for which AT&T provides wireless service and support. Early results have been mixed, but that union could prove to be a powerful synergistic partnership. The global automobile industry has also seen its share of co-opetition. NUMMI (New United Motors Manufacturing, Inc.), a pioneering joint venture of General Motors and Toyota established in the mid-1980s, has produced a number of successful vehicles including the Toyota Corolla and the Pontiac Vibe.

Peugeot and Toyota joined forces to produce a European "city car" in 2005. Although Ford owns Mazda and Volvo, those three companies have generally charted their own courses until rather recently, when they systematically shared capabilities to create a new generation platform that is based on their respective strengths: the hugely successful Mazda3.

This chapter has focused on information as the key to understanding and dealing with competitors, and for good reasons. Most companies seem able to devise useful competitive strategies, but many base those strategies on insufficient competitive knowledge, faulty assumptions about their competitors and their customers, and unsound competitive analysis that does not adequately consider each and every competitor. Whenever you hear talk about how to deal with "the competition," you should take a step back and ask, "which competitors," and then begin the process of acquiring credible information about them.

NOTES

1. For additional information on co-opetition, please see Adam M. Brandenburger and Barry J. Nalebuff, *Co-opetition* (New York: Doubleday, 1996).

TEN

Public Relations for Managers

Let us compare and contrast PR (public relations) actions of two executives in the wake of events that positioned their respective companies squarely in the bright lights of the national media. One got it right and one appears to have gotten it wrong.

JOHNSON & JOHNSON

James Burke was the CEO of Johnson & Johnson when, in 1982, seven people in the Chicago area died after ingesting extra-strength Tylenol capsules which were found to be poisoned with cyanide. Unsure about how widespread the contamination might be, public panic ensued and Tylenol's 35 percent share of the over-the-counter analgesic market plummeted. One individual with no known connection to Johnson & Johnson was found to have been responsible for lacing the product, but the damage to Tylenol's reputation had been done and the company's profits and market value tumbled. Many industry experts predicted that the value of the Tylenol brand would evaporate.

Burke could have opted for a defensive approach, riding out the storm caused by the scare and pointing out rightly that the contamination was an isolated act by a deranged individual. Instead, he went on the offensive, ordering a recall of some thirty million bottles of Tylenol and launching a massive PR campaign to inform the public. To win its confidence back, Burke became the face of Johnson & Johnson, appearing on every news and talk show that would book him, and speaking candidly about the scare. When a similar Tylenol tampering situation occurred in New York in 1986, Johnson & Johnson acted quickly. It halted production of the capsules (producing tablets and caplets instead), ordered a total nationwide recall of the capsules from all retail outlets, introduced new tamper-resistant packaging that would later become the standard in the industry, offered incentives to lure its customers back, and initiated an information drive to educate the public about the situation and the measures the company was taking to ensure that it never happened again.

The cost was high—around $200 million, not to mention the loss in the company's share price that accompanied the scare. However, Tylenol quickly gained much of its market share back and Johnson & Johnson won praise for its quick action on behalf of consumers. Some evidence even suggested that the company was rewarded by consumers who switched to Tylenol from other painkillers because they were reassured that the company did all that it could to protect their health and safety. Burke's actions helped the company achieve the status of consumer champion, a remarkable turn of events. To this day, his response to both Tylenol scares is regarded as a textbook example of how to handle a crisis.

MURRAY ENERGY CORPORATION

Although some executives appear to have learned from those events, others, unfortunately, seem to have learned nothing. Much to his credit, Robert Murray, owner of Cleveland, Ohio, based Murray Energy Corporation, arrived on scene within hours of the August 2007 coal mine collapse at his company's Crandall Canyon Mine in Utah that had trapped six miners. From the outset he took control not only of the rescue operation, but PR as well.

Things started to unravel for him fairly quickly after that. The eventual deaths of the miners and three members of a rescue crew were not the only disasters that happened at the mine. The general public's introduction to Murray occurred at his first postcollapse press conference, during which he discussed himself, his company, and those who have attacked or would attack his industry, criticized members of Congress for their participation in legislation restricting coal-mining operations, and lashed out at environmentalists in general. That all took place during a lengthy and, given the circumstances, entirely inappropriate diatribe in defense of the coal industry and its essential role in providing economical energy for citizens of our country whose insatiable appetite for electricity had to be met. He finally got around to mentioning the trapped miners approximately seven minutes into his speech.

In a subsequent press conference, he argued that the cause of the mine collapse was an earthquake, despite contrary seismographic evidence that suggested the collapse was triggered by a major "bump" resulting from pressures greater than the mine's coal pillars could withstand. At one point he also demanded (unsuccessfully) that members of local law enforcement clear news helicopters from the local airspace. All the public really wanted to hear from him was what his company was doing to save the trapped miners, details about the extent of the rescue operation that involved drilling hundreds of feet down into the ground, and what was being done to help the miners' families during that most difficult time. By ignoring those simple questions, and instead plowing ahead with his agenda when he had the spotlight, Murray's PR performance became a fiasco.

Burke's handling of the Tylenol scare was a masterpiece. He appeared calm and in control of himself and the situation at all times. He didn't attempt to stonewall, he acknowledged the problems, he stated the facts, he did not attempt to shift blame, he did more than what was legally required, he accepted social responsibility on behalf of his large company, and he proactively took the initiative to design safer medicine containers for the public good.

Murray, on the other hand, was defensive and combative, he obfuscated what had happened, he denied responsibility on the part of his company for the collapse despite evidence that the mine had experienced major "bumps" preceding the tragedy that should have served as a warning that its supporting coal pillars were under considerable stress, he changed the topic from the disaster to everything but the disaster, he attacked critics and opponents both real and imagined, and he failed to step up and commit his company to anything other than what appeared to the general public to be a rather disorganized effort to locate and rescue the trapped miners.

After a series of rescue attempts failed, and it was apparent to all that there were no miners alive to rescue, Murray simply vanished and allowed government mine safety officials to make whatever public statements were necessary. An examination of Murray Energy's history of mine safety violations and a review of Murray's personal statements to Congress during his lobbying against global warming laws, his anti-Union remarks and activities, his repeated attempts to intimidate anybody who stood in the way of his industry and his enterprise, and the fact that he subsequently filed lawsuits against several individuals who opposed him or gave opinions contrary to his during the events described above provides us with some insight as to why he might have reacted as he did.

PUBLIC RELATIONS 101

If you knew nothing about either of those two executives other than how they responded to their respective crises, for whom would you prefer to work? The importance of effective PR cannot be overstated, and how an organization responds to a crisis reveals a lot about it.

We have both good and bad news. Every employee in your organization represents your organization. Yes, that includes the supervisor who got into a fight in a local nightclub last Saturday night, the secretary who was elected chair of a community fundraising campaign, the accountant who stole money from a child's Little League team, and the executive who is known for philanthropy. Who has to handle the bad publicity? Usually all PR are handled by an executive or the manager of PR. But in the absence of either, publicity might have to be handled by any manager who is available. It probably is not a coincidence that bad things often happen when the people who usually handle these things are gone. Although large organizations usually have PR departments, and managers are instructed to send all media and community questions to the PR staff, most small companies do not have PR specialists.

In other words, there is a good chance that you will be handling PR, at least for your department if not for the entire organization. And chances are that you have never received any training in this area, which is true for most of us. Assuming that you fit into this category, one thing is critical. You must understand the philosophy driving media relations in your company. In other words, does your organization always take a "We will get back to you with a statement," position even when it has the facts? Or does your organization always come forward immediately with the honest facts that they have and offer to answer any questions? Or does your company land somewhere in between depending on the type of situation? If you clearly understand how the CEO wants these situations to be handled before they occur, the messenger (that would be you) is less likely to be shot.

Another aspect of PR is defining the organization's public. In other words, will information about your company be of interest to the national, regional, or local media? That depends on the type of news. Here are examples of types of information which will likely catch the attention of each level of media.

National media: former employee's attack on workers at the company's facility, fire in the facility resulting in deaths of workers and/or customers, the failure of a product that results in deaths, or, on a positive note, a visit by the president, a presidential candidate, or a major public figure. Except for the planned visit scenario, there is virtually no way to prepare for major unexpected events except to clearly understand who and how the CEO wants this type of PR handled before it happens. Of course, very few companies ever project a need to handle this type of crisis, let alone deal with the media. That can be said for events of even regional and local import.

Regional media: layoffs of employees, building a new plant, environmental accident, or facility visit by people from another country.

Local media: summer internship program for low income teen-agers, CEO chairing a local fundraising campaign, closure of the business due to a chemical spill, or the death of an employee in the plant.

Note that the more tragic the news, the broader the interest. The broader the scope of public interest, the more damaging the PR can be if handled improperly. It is flatly untrue that all publicity is good publicity for organizations. In fact, just the opposite is often true. Many organizations go bankrupt after an unfavorable story is released, especially if people become sick or die. Two well-known examples have to do with restaurant chains: Chi Chi's (a death resulted from eating bad onions at a store in Pittsburgh) and Sisters (*60 Minutes* did a story on how chicken is dangerous to eat if not cooked properly. Although Sisters was never mentioned, the chicken restaurant chain—a subsidiary of Wendys—went under within a year). The bad publicity associated with Martha Stewart's insider trading conviction and ImClone hurt that company despite promising research showing that its scientists might find a cure for cancer.

EMPLOYEES AS NEWS LINKS

When are your employees your public? Always! Too many managers do not consider their employees important in terms of managing impressions. Making sure that employees are fully informed about every situation that occurs and management's position allows them to feel safe at work and secure in their employment. It also provides them with information to share with their neighbors, friends, and relatives. You can submit a press release to the media, but your employees are also "releasing" infor-mation including the rumors and biases they add as the story develops. "Reliable sources" are usually employees. Ill-informed employees cannot be held accountable for distributing incorrect information. At least, well-informed employees can give the correct information if they so choose.

By the way, who are the employees who take negative stories to the media? You might guess ex-employees, people passed over for promotions, and other malcontents. You would be partially right, but you would have also overlooked a large contingent of other employees who also take information and rumors to the media. We have found that executives are often the worst offenders, in part because they have so much information at their disposal. Even though employees frequently tell family members, notably spouses, things that they do not want disseminated, spouses talk, sometimes deliberately and sometimes by accident. There is a reason that posters during World War II reminded people that "Loose lips sink ships."

In addition, your community is made up of potential employees. It is critical that you make a good impression on future applicants for jobs as well. Research has shown that when an organization has a high number of dissatisfied employees it is harder to recruit new employees.

BE TOTALLY HONEST

One key to dealing with negative events is honesty. It is critical that your responses to media and community questions be accurate. Despite all of the evidence regarding the consequences of lying to the media, not to mention the courts, managers still lie to the public. This issue probably has more to do with human behavior than business behavior, but lying never works. On the other hand, it makes people mad and then they are more likely to want to catch the manager or "the company" in the lie. We should have learned from history that the cover up is always worse than the transgression. Can you say "Watergate"?

DESIGNATE A SPOKESPERSON; HIRE A PR FIRM

When something bad happens, an appropriate person in the organization (the CEO will determine who that should be) should gather facts and develop a concise and complete explanation of what occurred, why it occurred, what the organization is doing about it, and what the organization is doing to ensure that this event never happens again. Make sure that the statement indicates that further investigation may reveal additional problems which will be addressed and explained as the work continues. And then follow up as that is done.

It is always good form to hire an outside firm or agency to assist in your investigation of problems. The name of the third party who will do the investigation should be shared with the public.

Be careful about "spinning" the news story to make the organization look better. Most of us can smell spin as it approaches us. The polished and cool image that a little spin can project is outweighed by a less sophisticated, but honest and sincere version of the truth. It is possible to hire PR specialists who can help you beat the bad news, but you must carefully consider the approach that you want to use. As we said earlier, we advocate an up-front management style where secrets are not hidden and facts are not manipulated.

Note that we said that the statement of what occurred should be concise. Here is an example of "less is more." There is no need to provide a communication overload. Often, we have a tendency to provide too much information so that the reporters and ultimately the public will "understand" our side of the story (i.e., why we could not have anticipated and prevented it), but that is a waste of time. You simply bring up more material for your attackers to use against you. Keep the information short, to the point, and accurate. Remember that the public is concerned with how this event will affect them personally. Write your press release from the standpoint of helping the public understand how it happened to others and how you are working to make sure that it does not happen to them.

Admit to what was done incorrectly, but do not admit guilt for negative consequences that are truly beyond the limits of your control. For example, several years ago a bus crashed and all of the passengers were killed. It was found that the driver was drunk. As if that was not bad enough, the press learned that the driver had been fired from previous jobs due to drunkenness. The company spokesperson admitted that they had not checked the driver's past work record. The spokesperson, however, did not say that the bus company was guilty of killing the passengers.

Note the difference. You may need to apologize—do that sincerely, but be careful not to apologize for something over which the organization had no control, such as killing passengers.

It is always best to be on the offense regarding negative publicity. If you know that something happened which will make the news, it is best to go out first and give the facts. Outing the company's problem is better than being caught. When this is done, do not withhold information that is relevant to the case. That is tantamount to lying. As we said before, admitting that engineers suggested that the bridge be replaced soon is quite different from admitting that the highway department killed people.

TOUT GOOD NEWS

We have been focusing on negative PR so far because that is what causes problems for us. Let's switch gears now. Suppose that one of your employees wins an award for community service, participates in the Olympics, or saves a life. Again, it is appropriate to release a statement offering congratulations to "our employee" who earned this achievement. You may want to include information about how long the individual worked for your organization and any role that the company played in the honor. Be careful not to let your organization take credit for that person's accomplishments unless credit is due. This is the kind of PR which is good and may rub off on the public's image of the organization. If your company has the highest United Way participation rate in your community, it is important to let your customers know that your employees are giving back. A press release is an inexpensive way of getting positive PR.

There are many ways to stage positive PR events. Much of that can be done through community leadership, which is explored in detail in the next chapter.

We advocate conducting PR drills as part of management training. Create a hypothetical situation and test each department manager on how she will handle the situation. Teach your managers and employees how to handle emergencies and the PR aspects of them.

PLAN NOW FOR CATASTROPHES

It is essential to have contingency plans for foreseeable major catastrophic events that might happen to or occur within your organization, and your PR response should be built into those plans. If you are a manager of a nuclear power plant, this is obvious, but what if you were the general manager of a bakery and an oven exploded, killing one of your bakers? Or what if you were a manager at a financial services company and one of your employees was escorted from your office in full view of a noontime crowd by federal marshals because she became involved in insider trading? These scenarios are "reputation busters," and they deserve a quick, measured response to contain the damage to your organization's image.

Think about the worst event that could happen to your organization and write a script to follow if it did. That way, you and your employees would have something to guide your actions (and words) when and if it did occur. People do not generally respond well in emergency situations; their thinking becomes rigid and they resort to a few responses that are familiar to them but that might not be appropriate given the circumstances. Help everybody do the right thing (you included) by writing down specific instructions to be followed. Then think about the next worst event and do the same thing. Then the next worst event. If you do that, you will be well prepared to handle emergencies as well as their PR aspects. You cannot have a contingency plan for everything, but if you cover several low probability critical events, and several higher probability important events, you should be set. You have the start of a preplanned response, which is far better than making things up as you go along.

One final word on PR: be very careful about judging the events that occur to other organizations. For example, if you are interviewed about something that happened to a competitor, be cautious about saying things like, "That never could have happened at XYZ because we do not take chances when it comes to our customers." The higher the pedestal on which you place yourself, the further you have to fall. Be gracious and express sympathy for the people affected by the situation.

ELEVEN

Community Leadership

Corporate citizenship is a term commonly used in management circles. It refers to the responsibility that corporations and their leaders have to their community. The term community has evolved from a focus on the local to the global for most organizations, but that depends on the organization's size and scope. In this book, we are focusing specifically on what individual managers can and should do. Most of you will be actively involved at the local level. Indeed, the bumper sticker which says, "Think globally, act locally" makes the most sense for most of us.

COUNTER THE STEREOTYPE

There is a tremendous amount of negative publicity regarding corporate America. The implication is that businesses (i.e., the executives) must make up for all the bad things that they do by giving away money. Sometimes, it seems like even the executives buy into this hype. The media, including television (both entertainment and news programming), movies, and newspapers are constantly displaying the worst behavior of executives of for-profit organizations. Business managers are represented either as idiots or evil manipulators. We, on the other hand, believe that most business managers are good honest people who do not owe their communities anything more than the jobs and economic development which they provide by doing business responsibly in a particular area. However, community leadership is important because, as American citizens, we do owe our families, friends, and neighbors life, liberty and the pursuit of happiness. As leaders in local organizations, we may have more leverage to provide the support and resources that can make a difference.

From a professional standpoint, it is important and valuable to develop a good reputation through community service. One of the ways to break into community work is to join the organizations which represent the causes most important to you. You may have groups to which you have belonged for years such as the Rotary Club, Lions Club, or Kiwanis. Different groups have different reputations in different communities. You need to check on this. For example, we can think of one national organization which is well known for providing support to veterans. However, in one of our hometowns, it was nothing more than a neighborhood bar populated by heavy drinkers. It is important to choose wisely which organizations will be worth your time and effort. You must do research and find out which local groups actually do good things and will help you to develop a positive reputation.

Given the enormous work load of most organizational leaders, it can be very difficult to choose which activities deserve your time and money. We suggest that you make decisions based on two criteria:

- One, what are your personal concerns and interests? For example, do you have a parent with a chronic illness like diabetes? Are you a musician? Do your children play sports? Put your time into the local groups which serve you and your family best.
- Two, which civic activities are consistent with the mission of your organization? For example, if you are the CEO of a hospital, the American Cancer Society would be an organization with consistent goals. If you are the vice president of a bank, a local program that teaches high school and college students how to use credit wisely would be a good choice. If you are the

superintendent of the school district, a tutoring program for disadvantaged children would make sense. In the long run, we suggest limiting your community service activities to one or two which allows you to put more time, money, and energy into those and do an exemplary job, instead of spreading yourself too thinly and doing a poor job with all.

THE BENEFITS OF DOING GOOD

One of the primary reasons for participation in community leadership is to develop a network with other leaders. Making friends while doing community service can be very valuable when working with other groups and in your career. You will meet other leaders who can provide connections, advice, and assistance for your next fundraiser. You will meet people whom you may want to hire to work for you in the future. You will meet people who may want to hire you in the future. You will also meet people who may want to buy a product your organization sells. Every contact that you make should be documented—name, address, phone number (work and cell), position, interests, employer, and special notes which may be useful later. For example, you may meet an employee services manager while working on the United Way campaign. You learn during a meeting that she used to work in sales and still has an interest in that. A year later, you have an opening in sales training. If you kept a file with names, titles, and information about others you meet in community service, you may have a candidate for your opening.

We have been talking primarily about working through local civic groups. There are other types of activities in which executives and middle managers are involved. In the previous paragraph, we mentioned the United Way campaign. This is a national campaign which takes place in every major city in the United States at the same time. Volunteer! Give money! In fact, you are expected to give your "fair share." Years ago, you would have been told specifically what your "fair share" was. You gave that. Today, you are "allowed" to decide how much you would like to give. Talk to your spouse, if you have one, and give generously.

Everyone knows what you are giving. How? All donors over $1,000 are tracked and recognized, in a brochure, by each local United Way agency. Depending on your level in your organization, you may be expected to be on that list or the list for the next level of giving. By the way, everyone who gives that much or more sees the list. You may be wondering why we mention the United Way, specifically. The reason is that corporate America has adopted the United Way as the primary cause—probably because it serves a variety of different agencies rolled into one campaign.

ASKED OR NOT, SERVE

If you are an executive in a large company, you may be asked to serve on a United Way (or other citywide campaign) committee. This is an honor, by the way. Only respected executives get asked. However, if you see an announcement in the paper or on the United Way Web site announcing the chair of the community campaign (usually a CEO of a large company), you can contact that person and volunteer to chair or serve on one of the committees. Usually, this involves attending meetings and being the public image for the campaign. It also means you are expected to give at a high level, which you will be doing anyway. If you are a middle manager and you volunteer and actively participate in the campaign, you will have exposure to every important CEO in your city. Lower-level managers are not expected to give at the same level as senior executives since your time is considered an important contribution. Your name will be placed in the newspaper and on fundraising materials. There can be important outcomes for you and your organization when you volunteer on major community-wide campaigns. Better committee assignments will come your way over time. Are we suggesting that you fake concern for your community by getting involved in the campaigns to advance your career? No. But if you do not care about your community now, start caring, and get involved.

As a senior executive, you may make decisions about how much time and money your organization will contribute to local groups. As mentioned earlier, this should be done based on the mission of the organization. Your personal interests should not drive corporate giving, just yours. List all of the fundraising campaigns that contact the organization and your organization's history of giving. Compare the level of giving with the mission of the organization. If there are conflicts between past giving and current priorities, make adjustments. Talk to other executives (internally and in some cases, externally as well), talk with corporate headquarters, if appropriate, and talk to the head of finance. Set a philanthropic budget and identify the levels appropriate for each campaign. The community and each group will expect you to increase your gift each year. We suggest that you notify a group if you are planning to cut or reduce your gift instead. You may also want to spread your giving over various types of organizations (e.g., the arts, children's groups, and health-related agencies).

You should use the same procedure to determine the amount of time which should be contributed. Many organizations provide loaned executives to work on campaigns. They may also allow employees to run special fairs, parties, and other fundraisers. How much time do you want your employees to spend on the campaign? Lots of activities often increase the amount of money that the employees give as a group. Is that important? Sometimes it is. For example, we work at a university that is supported by the local community and local leaders. They track our participation in the United Way campaign and expect us to give back to the community. Factor these types of considerations into your decision making. Involving promising employees in fundraising campaigns and community groups is an efficient way to develop leaders. It costs your organization very little and it can be fun and challenging for developing leaders and giving them broad community exposure. Many companies volunteer their best and brightest employees in order to give them practice leading. The organization gets more exposure and recognition too.

GREEN IS GOOD

A relatively new term in business is environmental stewardship. Unlike several years ago, there is little controversy these days about the need to preserve the environment. To be called a "tree hugger" is now a compliment. So what does this mean for managers? Simply, every single decision should be examined in an environmental context. When a new building is designed, the impact of the building on the environment should be assessed. Which location will have the least negative impact on the area's environment, flora and fauna? How can the negative aspects be limited? When evaluating current in-house procedures and systems, assess the impact on the environment. Can paper forms, for example, be eliminated? When a plant is being analyzed for efficiency, the impact on the environment should be assessed. Will efficiency upgrades require more electricity or push more pollutants into the air? Every decision has environmental implications. The goal today is to make decisions which will improve (at best) or not hurt the environment. Green is good and it is a growing movement.

Twenty years ago, if you met an environmental lawyer, he probably worked for a corporation and was hired to "deal" with the environmental groups and potential lawsuits. Today, large corporations are also likely to have an environmental engineer whose job is to ensure that better decisions are being made. If you happen to work for one of the large organizations with both environmental lawyers and engineers, use them. If you do not have those resources, hire consultants to give you educated opinions about changes, development, and construction projects. If you work for a small organization without a budget for consultants, become an expert on your own. Talk to the local environmental groups. Their members usually understand that change is inevitable, but they are happy to provide guidance and assistance with your planning. This may sound a lot like inviting the fox into the henhouse, but they know better than you do what the weaknesses of your changes are.

You may have noticed that we advocate an "up-front" or "out in the open" style of management. The instant you begin to try to fool people, from your employees to your bosses to community members to colleagues, you are doomed as a manager. Secrets backfire. Do not keep them, especially when it comes to issues which concern the general public. If you bring contentious issues out of the closet and openly discuss them, they are less likely to cause problems later. (Note that this cannot be done with personnel issues for legal reasons, but it can be done with environmental issues.) For example, if you want to expand the parking lot into an area where there is a stream bed inhabited by species of wildlife, it is better to bring this up and discuss it openly. Quietly expanding the lot, hoping that no one will notice, makes you look sneaky and manipulative to both employees and the community when the story breaks...as it surely will!

The bottom line is that environmental stewardship is simply a way of living now. Incorporate it into your everyday thinking and planning, model appropriate behavior to your followers and insist that it be built into all corporate decision making as a matter of course.

INVOLVE THE FAMILY

One of the biggest concerns about community leadership is the time that it takes. This means time away from work and time away from families. Managers are spending more and more time at work anyway. Volunteering on top of that can be a problem for your family. There is a simple solution and one which is very beneficial to the family as well as the community. Make the decision on which charities to support with your family. Make the choices personal. For example, many business leaders have chosen to volunteer and/or give to breast cancer agencies because their mothers or mothers-in-law have had breast cancer. Others choose the juvenile diabetes association because they have a child with the disease. Some will volunteer with the Girl Scouts if their children are members. When the entire family is involved, the time spent together is more worthwhile and sets an example for your children.

Fundraising can be fun. Find ways to raise money which includes family outings, picnics, trips to parks, and other outdoor settings. Children will remember the fun and the time with their parent, if not the fundraising. Events like "sock hops" give wives a chance to get their husbands on the dance floor and "balls" provide spouses an excuse to buy a new tuxedo or formal dress—not to mention the big night out. Friendly competitions like softball and volleyball games give everyone a reason to wear grungy clothes and interact informally.

Here are some tips regarding community leadership and your career:

1. Remember that you are being watched by your professional associates during community events. Drinking too much, sliding into a base to take out the another team's player, jumping semiclothed into your boss' pool, or dancing too closely with a friend's spouse will be noticed. It can hurt your career as well as embarrassing your family.

2. Managers often feel obligated to volunteer for their boss' favorite charity. A small donation given once per year can take care of this real or perceived obligation. Picking and supporting your own interests and needs will gain you respect and result in increased motivation on your part.

3. Political and religious fundraising can be touchy. Do not expect work colleagues to contribute to political parties or religious groups. It is appropriate for you to refuse to contribute to similar groups even when your boss proposes it. Many organizations have formed PACs (political action committees) administered by a company executive. The decisions about where the funds will go should be determined by what is best for the public, the company and the industry; however, a PAC can be used to direct contributions to specific candidates and political parties. Again, you have the right to refuse to contribute or ask for specifics regarding how the money is distributed. This may be difficult, but you should never be forced to contribute to candidates and issues that you do not support. This is illegal.

4. One issue which has recently become more important is criteria for membership to specific groups, even nonprofits. If you belong to groups that do not allow women or men or certain others to join, you limit your circle of acquaintances and the amount of good which can be accomplished by the group. For example, one community had a service group which supported

the local parks and the children's activities in the parks, including day and overnight camps. The group did fundraising and actually worked in the parks, cleaning, gardening, and maintaining the facilities. Only couples were allowed to join the group. When asked why only couples were allowed to join, the response was, "It has always been that way." The group had never thought about it before, but once they did, they changed their membership policy. Now, single people actively participate in the group. More money and time are contributed than ever before.

Obviously, there are much more sinister reasons for excluding some people from groups, but you do not want to be part of those. Belonging to civic groups which exclude others can be devastating to your career today. Most civic groups which used to be all male, like Kiwanis, are now coed. One way to be a community leader is to make it clear that you will not participate in any groups which still discriminate. Recently, much has been made of a policy by the Boy Scouts regarding who can be a pack leader. Different people see this differently. Use your best judgment when supporting any group with exclusionary policies.

Community leadership is important. Local professionals who give of their time and money often determine the viability of a community. This work will also contribute to the health and happiness of your family and those of your employees.

TWELVE

Bringing It All Together through Teamwork

We had initially thought to conclude this book with a chapter that integrated the preceding chapters, but decided against that for a couple of reasons. First, it would be very difficult to integrate such discrete topics as motivation, competition, and public relations in any meaningful sense. Second, we trust that our audience—you— is sophisticated enough to be able to understand our previous chapters without them having to be summarized for you.

We thus asked ourselves what the most popular trend in contemporary management is, and how we could present it in the context of selected material contained in our earlier chapters that pertain to every manager virtually every day. The popular trend was easy to identify—teamwork. Moreover, we consider teamwork in organizations to be *anything* but a fad. In the judgment of most experts, it is the wave of the future, for reasons that we will discuss. The material that we use to present the backdrop to demonstrate why teams are important and, simultaneously, how they can be most effective, was drawn from our chapters on goal setting, recruiting and selecting employees, motivating, communicating, and introducing and implementing change. You can understand and use work teams more effectively if you are aware of how the critical elements that affect team composition, processes, and performance, build on the topics that we presented earlier.

WHY ARE WORK TEAMS SO IMPORTANT?

Teams are increasingly being used by organizations to accomplish work that has traditionally been performed by individuals. We don't mean just assembling teams to perform specific onetime activities, which of course is quite common. We mean that many companies now use teams instead of traditional organizational structural units such as functional departments. There are a number of reasons why teams have become the fundamental organizational building block. Among other benefits that they provide to organizations, teams involve and empower employees to a far greater extent than traditional work units. They can cut across the hierarchy to get things accomplished more quickly and efficiently. They replace traditional levels of management and thereby reduce bureaucracy. Teams can be far more responsive to the needs and wants of customers. They can be tremendously flexible. And they can produce output of higher quality, and they can improve employee satisfaction, motivation, and productivity.

New product development, for example, is an activity that has realized tremendous gains through the use of work teams, which tend to develop innovations more quickly and reduce their time to market, with the result being more successful (i.e., profitable) product launches. As we will discuss, however, work teams also have their costs to organizations, and managers must be aware of both sides of the ledger when deciding whether and how to use teams to accomplish their objectives.

HOW PREVALENT ARE WORK TEAMS?

The list of companies that have switched to teams to accomplish large portions of their line operations reads like a who's who roster of U.S. industry: AT&T, Federal Express, General Electric, Honeywell, IBM, Procter & Gamble, Saturn, and Xerox, just to name a few. The big move in the 1990s to establish self-managed work teams was evidenced by well over half of the *Fortune 500* companies using teams as an essential element of their value creation processes. However, that trend has cooled off in recent years, because some companies that were originally hailed as success stories, such as Volvo, experienced a number of problems when they switched their entire production activities to teams. Many of the companies that attempted to imitate the success of early adopters of self-managed work teams, however, managed to eventually find the right balance, but the concept of *self-managed* work teams has given way to *managed* work teams. Yes, all of you managers are as relevant as ever.

WHAT ARE THE ATTRIBUTES OF WORK TEAMS?

In many organizations, the words "groups" and "teams" are used interchangeably. However, the actual differences between groups and teams are meaningful, so it is important that you understand them. Groups are sets of things. An assembly of you and your fellow managers, or you and your employees, or you and your friends, or even you and your family members, is a group. Teams are specific types of groups that have some special requirements, namely:

- Joint effort
- Interaction
- Coordination
- Synergy.

Teams are established to accomplish specific goals, whereas groups may or may not be. When we gather together in a coffee klatch, for lunch, as a book club, or during dinner together, we are a group. If we start working together during any of those gatherings, we might become a team—and perhaps just for that brief time. Generally, the goal of a group is to share information; the goal of a team is collective performance. Groups allow for individual accountability; teams require mutual accountability. The skill set of people in groups might be random and varied; the skills of team members are usually either the same or, often times, complementary.

Because organizations prefer to use the word teams almost exclusively, we will follow that convention in this chapter.

Groups tend to form naturally and informally, because human beings are social creatures. Groups provide us with strength in numbers and security, they provide us with mutual support both physically and emotionally, and they help us protect our identities or other facets of our being that are important to us. Professional organizations are good examples of groups. Teams, on the other hand, are usually carefully constructed and managed to get the most from peoples' respective capabilities, and are designed to achieve *synergy*.

WHAT IS ALL THIS TALK ABOUT SYNERGY?

Synergy is one of those words that is tossed around pretty indiscriminately these days, as if it were magic dust. Synergy essentially boils down to the equation $1 + 1 + 1 = 4$. What that means is that if three of us were to work individually and put our effort together, and each of us had a productive output of 1, then we would expect our productive output together to equal our additive individual efforts, or 3. However, if by working together, sharing information, and incorporating that additional information in our collective thought process, we achieve something more than our additive output; hence, 4. To illustrate synergy, just look at successful professional sports teams. All professional athletes possess superb talents, and the individual performance differences between teams are slight. More often than not, the teams that perform the best do not necessarily have all of the best "parts," but they have parts that are willing and able to function in a complementary way and they configure those parts better than their competitors. Just look at the Detroit Pistons, winners of the National Basketball Association championship in 2003–2004 and finalists in 2004–2005. Good but not great talent, excellent complementary skills, players who knew their respective roles and were not concerned with who had the ball the longest or scored the most points, willing to work together and do whatever it took to accomplish a single goal: win an NBA championship. The Pistons were a vivid example of synergy in action.

As a manager, how can you make sure that your teams develop synergy? By making sure that you have the right people on the teams and in the right positions. Synergistic teams make the most effective teams.

WHAT DO I NEED TO KNOW ABOUT THE DIFFERENT TYPES OF WORK TEAMS?

Perhaps you have found yourself assigned to a team. It might have been a committee of some sort, or a "tiger team" composed to handle a particularly thorny issue that required concentrated effort by managers of different units in your organization. Whether you experienced the joys or the frustrations of working on a team, you know an important fact that is sometimes overlooked by higher-ups who do the assigning: team effectiveness isn't just a function of its productive output, it is also a function of how satisfied the members of the team were during their tenure on the team. As social animals, people naturally form groups, but being assigned to a team violates our ability to make our own choices regarding with whom we surround ourselves. It is a good thing that we humans also adapt fairly well to changing circumstances when we must.

Effective teams, then, have a dual function: to produce a desired output and to keep members satisfied about being on the team so that they will continue to contribute productively. Let's set aside productivity for the moment and focus on satisfaction. Your employees would probably be most satisfied if they were assigned to teams with people who they know and people whose jobs are similar. That is the most natural tendency. We prefer to be in the company of people like us—people who look and talk like us, people who have been educated and trained like us, and people of roughly our same age and background. If teams are composed of such people, they are called *homogeneous* teams. Homogeneous teams are most effective when the goal is to focus tremendous functional expertise on an issue, or to maintain the status quo, or to fend off a threat. In homogeneous teams, conflict tends to be low and agreement tends to be high. Homogeneous teams have the added advantage of being able to implement solutions that they devise most effectively and efficiently. Ensuring that members of such teams are satisfied is not usually a major concern of the manager because people know why they are on the team and what is expected of them; they will feel as if they are all in it together.

However, in many cases, managers don't have the luxury of assigning people to homogeneous teams. More and more, organizations are taking advantage of the benefits of using *heterogeneous* teams—teams composed of employees from different functional areas or departments, with quite different backgrounds and experiences, and who speak a different "language" in their daily work lives. Heterogeneous teams have become popular because they can bring expertise from across an organization together in a quick, efficient way. Heterogeneous teams are most effective in situations where innovation is needed. Unlike homogeneous teams that are composed vertically, heterogeneous teams are assembled horizontally.

Cross-functional teams represent the classic example of heterogeneous teams. Cross-functional teams are made up of people from whatever parts of the organization are needed to bring the required skills to bear. On those teams it is essential to have complementary skills, so it is very likely that the members might not know each other or might never have worked with one another on a previous task. Heterogeneous teams are most appropriate when the need for change is high or a creative approach to some situation is warranted. In heterogeneous teams, the multiple perspectives that fly about, especially among strangers, result in less agreement among members because they usually feel little pressure to "keep the peace." Ironically, although the attributes of heterogeneous teams frequently result in innovative solutions, their very nature works against their ability to implement those solutions very effectively or efficiently. That is why managers matter. An additional challenge to you as a manager is that you must ensure that your employees who are assigned to heterogeneous teams experience satisfaction so that they will (a) contribute to the team's success, and (b) want to be a member of a similar team in the future. That is a tall order, and you need to understand the characteristics and dynamics of teams to be able to meet that challenge.

WHAT ARE THE CHARACTERISTICS OF EFFECTIVE WORK TEAMS?

In our experience, the most effective work teams have the right number of people playing the right parts. By "parts" we don't mean their functional expertise, which we mentioned in our discussion of heterogeneous teams. We trust that everybody can figure out what kinds of skills are needed. It is a more difficult issue to determine what kinds of roles people need to perform.

We are frequently asked, "What is the ideal size of a work team?" as if there were some magic number. When we say that we don't know, and ask people what they think, the answer we receive most frequently is "seven." Where that came from, we can only speculate—it is an agreeable number, some say a lucky number; it might be a vestige of management thinking from back in the early days of the industrial age, when organizations were told by the experts that the effective span of control for any manager was seven subordinates. Anyway, for your situation, it might in fact be seven. Or three. Or fifteen. The correct number is an unqualified "it depends."

Your work teams should be the *right* size, and that depends on their purposes and objectives. The right size falls between the minimum number required to bring the requisite skills to bear, and the maximum number that can work together and still enable each member to feel that they are an integral and essential member of the team. Ideally, those two limits will be the same. When in doubt, however, go smaller rather than bigger. The identity of your team members as individuals and collectively is absolutely essential to preserve if the team is to develop synergy and become as effective as possible.

There are two types of roles that team members must play, and most members play one or the other: task specialists and social facilitators. Task specialists are the real experts, or the technicians. Engineers make excellent task specialists, as do scientists, economists, and accountants. Social facilitators provide the glue that binds team members together and helps them resolve the inevitable conflicts that will occur when task specialists butt heads. In our experience, organizations always—we repeat, always—overstock teams with task specialists at the expense of social facilitators. That is natural, but if you want to manage a more effective team, then you must resist that temptation and assign people to fulfill both of those roles. Having said that, we fully recognize that a team consisting of a couple of task specialists and four or five social facilitators won't solve very many problems. The point here is to not underestimate the value of "people" people in assigning team members.

Research suggests that the best decisions are made by experts. Task specialists must have a large say in making decisions that involve their expertise directly. Others on the team will contribute to decisions when and where their expertise is involved. Social facilitators will provide feedback on how others outside the team will view the outputs of the team's work and how best to sell it to the organization.

We urge you not to assign a leader to your work team, and instead allow one to emerge naturally. Let the team members bestow that mantel on the person of their choosing. Who make the most effective team leaders? It shouldn't surprise you to know that those are the unique individuals who can fill a dual role—operating both as a task specialist *and* as a social facilitator. They might not possess the most expertise, or provide the strongest social glue, but they have a sufficient amount of each. Those people are rare in organizations, and if you identify them, hang onto them. They are respected by others and they are valuable.

A final role that is sometimes visible in work teams is not really a viable role at all. It is the nonparticipator. It is inevitable that on occasion somebody completely unsuited to the task gets assigned to a work team. Our advice to you is to identify that person as quickly as possible and remove them from the team immediately. Nonparticipators don't offer anything, and by their mere presence they will bring down the performance of the entire team. You cannot afford to let that happen.

We suggest strongly to you that you select team members with the utmost care and consideration—don't put weak members on teams and trust that they will somehow flourish. Work teams cannot be allowed to become a refuge for those few employees that you would like to isolate from the rest. Don't assign your overly assertive problem children to teams, either. Nobody enjoys work-ing with egotistical, arrogant know-it-alls, and the team to which they are assigned will suffer.

WHAT TEAM PROCESSES DO I NEED TO KNOW ABOUT?

The most effective work teams evolve largely on their own, and managers can't force things to happen on a fixed schedule or according to some master plan, or they might not happen at all. Good managers recognize this, and experienced managers follow the process closely but unobtrusively, making adjustments as needed with a light hand.

The first process that you must understand is that teams develop through several identifiable stages,[1] each of which requires time and internal adjustment. Here are those stages and what occurs during them:

- *Forming:* members become orientated and get acquainted with each other;
- *Storming:* personalities emerge, roles are defined, and conflict and disagreement occur;
- *Norming:* order is established by the team, cohesion is achieved, and a leader emerges;
- *Performing:* the problem receives the team's full attention and the task is accomplished;
- *Adjourning:* closure is realized.

The forming stage might take longer than you might expect, particularly if team members have not worked together in the past. Of course, that stage might be short if team members are familiar with one another.

Storming is essential, and managers who try to accelerate it or force agreement or consensus at this stage risk limiting the team's effectiveness without even knowing it. We recommend against exerting control from the outside. If you get involved with too much hands-on management, you will fool yourself into believing that you made everything all better.

Norming is a stage that actually occurs quickly, because the earlier stages set the stage for it. People want order at this point and will naturally work to achieve it. Again, we caution managers to monitor their team without taking control. By anointing a leader, you might be setting the team up for internal conflict that could hinder its performance.

Performing—finally! Why on earth does it sometimes take so long to get to this stage? Our answer: because it does; remember that you are dealing with people. We have found that managers expect work teams to settle right in and work the problem. That seldom happens. Some research has suggested that members of work teams have innate clocks and calendars in their heads, and they really start to dig in and work together when it becomes apparent that their deadline is looming.

Adjourning is a stage in the process that too few organizations take advantage of, and we consider it essential for you to take the time to help your work teams achieve closure. We all know what should happen if a work team fails to accomplish its assignment—we would conduct an autopsy or postmortem to see what went wrong so that we could take measures to ensure they won't in the future. But we seldom take the time to dissect what happens when work teams succeed and accomplish their assignment, and perhaps even other assignments that they took upon themselves to accomplish. Wouldn't you like to model that process and those behaviors for use in the future? Absolutely you would. So do it. Take the time to perform a detailed assessment of what went right and why. Further, it is also our experience that managers often take success for granted, and fail to determine how their work teams succeeded in spite of things that went wrong. It is fine to bask in the glory of success, but without properly identifying and analyzing things that could have led to failure, you risk having them derail your work teams in the future.

You need to understand how teams develop norms and cohesiveness. Norms are informal standards of conduct that members of teams share, and that guide their behavior. They commonly develop when events occur early in the team's history, or when people mention examples of norms that governed their behavior as a member of an earlier team, or when somebody makes an explicit statement that others rally around.

Cohesiveness is a measure of the degree to which team members are attracted to the team and motivated to serve it. Essentially, cohesiveness refers to the closeness or interpersonal attractions that exist between team members. Teams that demonstrate cohesion have members who develop social as well as work relationships with other team members, work as one to define their goals and objectives, downplay their individual differences and instead focus on their similarities, interact frequently and openly, and (if asked) prefer to be rewarded as a team instead of as individuals.

Here are some things that managers must understand. Ideal work teams are highly cohesive and develop norms in alignment with their organizations'. That is the best-case scenario, because those teams will be highly productive. They will succeed. But here is the rest of the story, and it might be counterintuitive. Cohesiveness is good, right? Not always! The least productive work teams are those that become highly cohesive and develop norms that are inconsistent or in opposition to those of their organizations. Why? Because they might resemble a close-knit country club. They get along just fine, they choose not to do more work or get to know other people, and they certainly don't welcome any outside "help."

As a manager, you face a real dilemma if a work team becomes out of control. By that, we mean a team that consistently opts for the obvious simple solution to a problem and fails to fully explore all ideas and possibilities. Such a team might also have developed inappropriate personal relationships which prevent team members from challenging each other. One thing that you could do is to assign another employee to the group with the hope of injecting some discipline into its view of the task at hand. If you decide to do so, you could assign a hard-charger, who might be able to stir the pot successfully, but who might be viewed with distrust or disdain by team members who have already established their own team identity. Alternatively, you might consider assigning somebody who is low-key but well respected, and who might have a better chance of fitting in and avoiding outright rejection. He or she might be able to help the team turn it around.

Another option would be for you to intervene when you see that cohesion/norm combination occurring. If you do so, you might consider bringing some backup with you so that the team will recognize the seriousness of the situation and, hopefully, the problems that they have created for themselves and you. Your meeting should be as open as possible, and should become an open forum for discussion. If team members have a say, there is a chance that they will come around and align themselves more closely with the overall organization. Another tactic that you might find effective would be to identify and remove from the team the person most responsible either for the tight cohesion (riskier) or the improper norms (less risky).

If nothing works, you face the dismal but necessary task of dismantling the team altogether, and reconstituting a new one. If that happens, you can use some of the original team members, but on different teams.

What if your work team's norms are fine but cohesiveness is low? Its productivity will be moderate, but it can be improved. You first need to determine why cohesion is low, then take the most conservative measures to help it improve. Perhaps the team is simply too large. If so, reduce its size. You could ask an outside facilitator to help by conducting training or a team building exercise. Another thing that you could do would be to assign a known social facilitator to the team. You should know who those people are; they are extroverts who seem socially connected to everybody in the organization. You could also hold a social gathering to give team members an opportunity to establish friendlier relations with one another. Other members of the team will probably appreciate your efforts to help out.

What if your work team's norms are incongruent with the organization's, but its cohesiveness is low? This is probably the easiest "problem" situation that you could face. The solution? Disband the team and try again. That is the simplest and most direct approach. Something isn't clicking and it would take more time and effort to diagnose and solve the problem than the effort is worth.

HOW DO I REWARD WORK TEAM MEMBERS?

How to reward members? That depends on how much discretion you are allowed. The simple answer is that to motivate them to work together as a team, they should be rewarded as a team. That goes especially for any bonus for which they would be eligible. Think about several of the problems described in the preceding section—could an inappropriate reward system have been a factor? If you want people to work together, and you reward them only for their individual contribution, then what do you expect? Options for rewards include incentives for cost savings and profit enhancement, and bonuses for increasing sales and reducing product returns.

WHY IS TEAM CONFLICT SUCH A BIG DEAL, AND HOW CAN I MANAGE IT?

Whenever people work together in teams, some conflict is inevitable. Some causes of conflict are individual—people experience stress that is unfamiliar to them, their familiar routines have been changed, they have to get used to how different people think and behave, there might be personality clashes, and power and status differences might get in the way of real progress. Some causes of conflict will be organizational—jurisdictional ambiguities caused by not knowing the limits of the team's authority and responsibility, being perceived as "special" by others who might become envious of the team, scarce resources, and communication breakdowns.

Managers can do several things to deal with team conflict:

- Open those lines of communication and ensure that they stay open. Be available to your work teams 24/7 to help facilitate their issues.
- Communicate on the team's behalf to others in the organization when appropriate.
- Mediate when asked or when you see that it is necessary—and don't wait until after the fact. Mediation is appropriate (a) within the team and (b) between the team and others, as the situation dictates.

- Provide the team with well-defined tasks to relieve members' uncertainty and provide them with a direction for their efforts.
- Negotiate and bargain as necessary to ensure that team members perceive that their efforts will be recognized and that they will be compensated accordingly.
- Establish superordinate goals—that is, goals that cannot possibly be accomplished without the effort of every member of the team. If everybody has to do her part, she will do it.

Some conflict will occasionally result from social loafing and free riding. When individuals feel that they are anonymous, or that others are available to solve problems, they have a tendency to withhold effort and assume that others will do the work. Additionally, some team members might be lazy and pretend to be busy while letting others cover the work. Social loafing and free riding can be avoided by assigning team members clearly defined individual responsibilities within the framework of their team responsibilities, and holding them accountable for those responsibilities. When people are idle, they should be given a task that is constructive and helps to move the team along towards its goals.

WHAT ARE SOME OF THE COSTS ASSOCIATED WITH USING WORK TEAMS?

We discussed some of the benefits at the beginning of this chapter: high effort, member satisfaction, synergy, speed, organizational flexibility, enhanced productivity, and others. We also mentioned some of the problems that can occur, but we need to discuss more about the costs of using work teams.

Work teams require effort to manage. Managers need to pay close attention to what is happening without becoming too involved—a delicate balancing act. After all, if you jump in and start running your work teams, they will stop functioning as teams and allow you to do everything, which defeats the purpose of establishing them.

Work teams are especially difficult to coordinate when they are comprised of individuals from multiple units; they require managers around the organization to communicate openly and frequently to ensure that their employees assigned to the team are being appropriately utilized. The existence of work teams can result in some power realignments in your organization, and that causes problems for managers and potentially many other employees.

Collective bargaining agreements should be considered carefully if your organization is unionized and you wish to assign union members to work teams that have not been acknowledged explicitly in labor agreements. Cooperative working relationships with your unions are essential in those cases.

Work teams can experience "risky shift," which means that they might engage in more risky behavior collectively than any of their members would individually. The reason for that is that it is difficult for management to pinpoint individual responsibility for work team decisions. If work team members know that they will receive significant compensation if they hit a home run, they will swing for the fences. Unfortunately, that means that they might strike out more often than they would had they been trying to hit a single—which might have been management's goal all along.

Work teams are very susceptible to "groupthink," or the tendency for team members to be more interested in achieving consensus and harmony than exploring alternatives, hashing it out, and making more enlightened decisions about their goals and what it will take to accomplish them. Groupthink occurs when discussion and consideration of additional information is limited early on. You need to know that groupthink is especially prevalent when work teams are homogeneous and highly cohesive, because team members can start to believe that they know it all or will be impervious to any criticism or negative consequences for their actions.

Managers can prevent or mitigate the effects of groupthink. One way is to appoint a Devil's advocate to every work team. That person might not be a team member, but should meet with the group periodically to question members about their rationale, present them with counter arguments, enlighten them about the organization's position and goals, etc. Another tactic is to reward team members who openly debate the issues or present information that others have not considered. The most powerful way to counter groupthink, of course, is to hold each team member accountable for the team's decisions and actions. That is why members of juries are asked individually whether they support the panel's findings.

WHAT ARE SOME CURRENT TRENDS IN WORK TEAMS?

The major trend is that they are here and they are being used with increasing frequency in all types of organizations. Work teams have become an organizational fact of life. Other than their sheer rise in popularity, one major trend in work teams that we observe is that they are becoming more diverse in many ways—spanning more disciplines and including more generations of workers than ever before. Part of that is being driven by the presence of aging baby boomers and the recent influx of young talent in so many organizations. Diverse teams have a number of advantages over less diverse teams, some of which we mentioned briefly in our discussion of heterogeneous teams, including wider breadth of experience and expertise, multiple perspectives, enhanced creativity, more learning opportunities, and a greater ability to perform internal "reality checks."

We caution you, however, to be careful about your assumptions about what "diversity" means. Easily identifiable dimensions of diversity such as sex or race are often important determinants of differences, to be sure, but they can also be misleading. Less visible dimensions such as personality, experience, and education are often more important in determining our diversity, and people's core values, beliefs, and cultural backgrounds *really* shape their uniqueness. We encourage you to think about those facts when you assign your employees to work teams.

There are two special challenges that confront diverse work teams. First, the potential for conflict is greater, while achieving cohesion and productivity can be more difficult. Second, all things being equal, people of like backgrounds prefer to stick together and remain apart from those with different backgrounds. Our affiliation preferences are quite persistent. We have mentioned these two truths previously, but they bear repeating because of their amplified effect on diverse teams.

FINAL THOUGHTS

First, we have discussed assigning your employees to teams throughout this chapter, as if that is the only way that they would become members of work teams. We recommend that sometimes you allow them to select themselves for membership on your work teams. Some people naturally prefer the social interaction and give-and-take characteristic of energetic teams, so they would make far better candidates than people who would prefer to sit at a desk in the corner, tucked away in relative obscurity.

Second, simply bringing together people who share a common goal and an enthusiasm for the process might not result in effective teamwork or yield the expected results. It is the manager's responsibility to set goals, monitor progress, and work with the team to solve problems.

Third, there is no one-size-fits-all template for effective team development. Every situation is unique, and managers need to know that the best thing they can do is to gather as much information as they can, assign the right people to the best of their ability, communicate frequently, monitor progress, look for problems, and intercede quickly but delicately to help work teams along.

Fourth and finally, work teams do not equal or substitute for effective management. Managers need to actually manage work teams, and they must do so with a deft hand.

NOTES

1. Bruce W. Tuckman, "Developmental Sequence in Small Groups," *Group Facilitation: A Research and Applications Journal* 3 (Spring 2001): 66–81.

Index

About the Authors

PEG THOMS is Professor of Management and Director of the MBA Program in the School of Business at Penn State Erie, The Behrend College. She is the author of *Project Leadership from Theory to Practice* (1998), *Driven by Time* (Praeger, 2003), and *Finding the Best and the Brightest* (Praeger, 2005), as well as the co-editor of *Battleground: Business* (Praeger, 2007). She has conducted extensive consulting, leadership development, and training programs with organizations in both the public and private sectors.

JAMES F. FAIRBANK is Associate Professor of Management at Penn State Erie, The Behrend College. A graduate of the U.S. Naval Academy and a Navy veteran, he is the author of numerous journal articles and has done extensive management consulting and training.